LOOKING THROUGH YOU

By the same author

Poetry
Sheltering Places
The Lundys Letter
Sunday School
Heart of Hearts
The Morning Train
Lake Geneva
Points West
Selected Poems
Mickey Finn's Air
The Last Peacock

Prose

The Proper Word
Catching the Light
Of War and War's Alarms
In Another World
The Wrong Country
The Sound of the Shuttle

As editor

The Younger Irish Poets
Earth Voices Whispering
The Cambridge Companion to Irish Poets

LOOKING THROUGH YOU

Northern Chronicles

GERALD DAWE

With photographs by
Euan Gébler

MERRION
PRESS

First published in 2020 by
Merrion Press
10 George's Street
Newbridge
Co. Kildare
Ireland
www.merrionpress.ie

9781785372810 (Cloth)
9781785372827 (Kindle)
9781785372834 (Epub)

A CIP catalogue record for this book is
available from the British Library.

Typeset in Sabon 11/15 pt

Cover photograph courtesy of Bobbie Hanvey.

Merrion Press received financial assistance from The Arts
Council for this publication.

Merrion Press is a member of Publishing Ireland.

Printed in Great Britain by TJ International Ltd

For Dorothea

At certain periods of history, it is only poetry that is capable of dealing with reality by condensing it into something graspable, something that otherwise couldn't be retained by the mind.

Joseph Brodsky, *Less Than One*

LIST OF ILLUSTRATIONS

CONTENTS

PREFACE

There was a warren of sheds and yards wedged in behind the backs of the houses in an urban island between two well-stocked avenues of traditional red-brick family homes in north Belfast. I knew the district well. Friends lived there, there were shops we all visited for 'messages', a delicatessen and hairdresser, and long-gone stores like Roycroft's and Billy Duddy's. But in the 1940s this little annex had been part of the extensive preparations throughout Northern Ireland for the US Army and 'D' Day. My uncle and his mates as young teenagers used to cadge Lucky Strikes and chewing gum from the GIs passing through by war's end. Farther down, along the shore side, prefabricated houses had been built to accommodate many hundreds of people as a result of the Belfast Blitz in 1941. Others, returning home from evacuation, found, billeted in their homes, officers en route to the European battlefields.

When I was about nine years old this district became my stamping ground, as Richard Burton's magisterial voice-over was broadcast on the BBC's *The Valiant Years* (1961), Churchill's history of World War II. Ex-servicemen could be seen in their ceremonial blazers heading off to the local serviceman's club, the British

Legion. Our house retained the black-out blinds and I recall empty ration books in a press. War was general. Whether we liked it or not, World War II and its legacies influenced much of what happened in the 1950s and well into the 1960s, if not beyond. Behind that wartime screen of film, dress and demeanour, the voices and lifestyles of an older generation played out its own declining destiny.

'Uncle' Oswald, a close friend of my grandmother, loved accompanying on piano her singing and recitations of verse; with his dapper Aquascutum overcoat and short dashing moustache, he wheezed, at times badly, as a result of a German gas attack at the Front. When I worked for a time in Belfast's Central Library on Royal Avenue, a tall spindly older man would often be seen across from the library steps addressing skywards in a clipped Northern Anglo tone where 'Monty' (General Montgomery) and his troops were moving on an imaginary map. El Alamein, I think it was. Sitting outside the Arcade bar downtown most Saturdays, a partially sighted veteran played a harmonica and sought alms from those busily heading to the cinema, pubs and dancehalls.

Relics of wars – statues, regimental flags, commemorative plaques outside churches, remaining blitzed sites – the whole business of destruction, sacrifice and loss were embedded in that civic world. So it is really no surprise that in the back bedroom, which was my retreat from all this, the wall next to my bed was covered with other symbols, very different signs of the time.

At first it was English football league tables with little name tags which you could move up and down according to the Saturday results, alongside a double spread of the team I supported (Spurs). This was soon to be replaced as motorcycles gleamed in all their polished power – AJS, Honda, Suzuki. And you could readily imagine riding those mighty machines, with their all-consuming engine sound, because at the weekends leather-clad young men and their girlfriends shot past our house on their way to TT races, or their versions of them, on the hilly avenues above us leading towards Belfast Castle. If you were out walking along the Shore Road you could hear the music pumping out of a little café where the rockers hung out. It was all a little bit too much for me; I don't know why. But then The Shangri-Las were mourning for 'The Leader of the Pack' and Twinkle's 'Terry' hit of 1964 was blasting out too, a strange, lurid, death-haunted song which became known by genre as a teenage tragedy song: 'He rode into the night, accelerated his motorbike / I cried to him in fright, don't do it, don't do it, don't do it.' One afternoon, just below us, a young motorcyclist, attempting to overtake a van on the rising camber of the road, was struck by an oncoming lorry and died instantly. Before his funeral, fellow bikers arrived in numbers and circled before placing their right boots at the very spot.

From then the bikes disappeared from my wall and the faces of my burgeoning musical heroes of the time appeared in their place and would take over my teenage years. Cream, Jimi Hendrix and the Small

Faces became not only figures in magazines, heard on the transistor radio and seen on the black and white TV, they were 'live' in the various clubs and venues in downtown Belfast.

But first it was The Beatles. I recall sitting on the bus home from Orangefield, my new school across town, as a solitary and temporarily liberated cow went blattering down Donegal Square, along by the front of the City Hall. It was a bizarre sight indeed for busy-busy work-a-day Belfast, but off it went – into May Street and beyond. Later that night, as we sat having our tea, I mentioned what I saw earlier that day. 'It's because The Beatles are here; someone's done that for publicity', my mother interjected without rhyme or reason. It was 1963. The Beatles were indeed in Belfast.

Looking Through You begins there and then, listening to The Beatles and becoming aware of the shift in gear which *Rubber Soul* heralded: a more complicated lyric for a more questioning world. What followed was the discovery of inspirational American poets such as Robert Lowell and Sylvia Plath, the movement in and out of my Protestant background, life and reading in the early years of the Troubles, and some of the poems which I produced about those challenging and changing times.

Gerald Dawe
Belfast
February 2020

ONE

I was eleven when The Beatles started their inexorable rise to global fame in 1963 and eighteen when they split up. So there's a slight hitch in the way one thinks about that past because it isn't separate or 'other'; it is, as Stewart Parker, Irish playwright and one-time 'High Pop' columnist for *The Irish Times*, had it, 'bred in the bone', remarking in 1976 on the re-release by EMI of all The Beatles' singles – 'it is a new and sobering experience, to see the music of your adolescence revived as though it were something historical and unfamiliar rather than something bred in the bone'.

To think aloud about *Rubber Soul* or *Revolver* or *Sgt. Pepper's Lonely Hearts Club Band* is to take in the time when one first heard the albums, and with whom and where. An emotional mosaic unselfconsciously surfaces through the lyrics and the music, along with the unmistakable merging harmonic of the voices. It all adds up to an indefinable atmosphere of what it felt like once to hear the words that one knew, *we* knew, by heart. Because The Beatles' songs *were* all known by heart.

It amazes me to this day just how many songs, moves and air-guitar moments reside in all my sixty-plus-something friends' heads and gestures half a century on. We watched the at-times snowy black and white TV screen or listened, as pop-pickers, to the radio (and transistors) and obsessed over LPs, singles and EPs in the record shops of Belfast's city centre and hung out in the *casbah* known as Smithfield, before taking the step into one of the many clubs and dance halls that were such a feature of downtown Belfast before the desperate days of the Troubles.

In passing, it might be worth noting that when *Rubber Soul* came out at the beginning of 1965, that year also marked an auspiciously hopeful – albeit short-lived – moment in local history with the first meeting since December 1925 of an Irish Taoiseach, Seán Lemass, and the Prime Minister of Northern Ireland, Terence O'Neill. The meeting took place on 13/14 January. Not that it caught the imagination of the teenagers with whom I was hanging out in downtown Belfast.

Listening to The Beatles was part of listening to a widening circle of groups for my part of that sixties' generation – slightly too young to see The Beatles perform live in the Ritz cinema in 1963 or the following year in the King's Hall; *listening* to their albums was what we did. Indeed, I have a notion – which could well be completely wrong – that this is what we mostly did with The Beatles' music, throughout their ascendancy and into the post-Beatles decade of the seventies and beyond: listen and not dance to it. For though dancing was such a part and parcel of our social life, there were few enough Beatles songs that I can recall actually *dancing* to other than with the slower 'smoochier' numbers. This was distinctly different to the free-forming individualistic moves that accompanied The Rolling Stones' records, or the shifting macho showings-off to all the excellent R&B bands that performed in Belfast, as well as the personal favourites of my own cohort of friends, such as the Small Faces, who got everyone going, even at their so-called sit-down 'concerts', from the very first beat of Stevie Marriott's pouting, knock-kneed skip across the stage of the Ulster Hall.

My first recollection of listening to The Beatles – once they had broken through the great sound barrier with their earlier albums – is hazy. My sister may well have had those early albums like *With The Beatles* or *A Hard Day's Night* – and screamed along with her friend from the sofa at The Beatles' televised performances in what Dominic Sandbrook calls, in *Never Had It So Good: A History of Britain from Suez to The Beatles*, their 'smart grey lounge suits from Burton's, with velvet collars and thin lapels' on ATV's *Sunday Night at the London Palladium*. There were also those 'North of England accents' which, in Sandbrook's view, 'immediately associated [The Beatles] with honesty, dynamism and authenticity'. The lads seemed to be like neighbours' boys – unaffected, unpretentious but smartly mocking. It is *Rubber Soul* which lodges in my mind as the first real logging of what The Beatles meant beyond the screams and the TV shows, but the impact also had, initially, a lot to do with hair, about which I will quickly explain.

After my uncle was demobbed from the RAF in 1962 or thereabouts, he stayed with my mother, my sister and me until he sorted out what he would do and where he would go. Along with his best pal, Carly, he took me one day to his barber, a very well-known barber in the docklands of lower northside Belfast, whose regulars included famous and infamous locals such as the Tiger's Bay hero Buck Alec (who reputedly kept a lion as a pet, along with snakes), boxers, weightlifters, actors and the like. I emerged from this barber one bright Saturday afternoon with my hair quiffed up like a newly risen loaf and sat, between both 'uncles', on the 64 bus home, alienated from the face that was staring back at me in the bus driver's rear window.

For that face bore the look of the fifties' crooners my uncles impersonated, or they might have had in mind someone like Hank Marvin of The Shadows, though I doubt that. Either way, the association with the smooth sounds that emanated from the gramophone my uncle bought for the family house and on which he played Nat King Cole, Frank Sinatra, Peggy Lee and soundtracks from films like *The Eddie Duchin Story*, was simply a bridge too far.

When I arrived home, I walked straight towards the bathroom upstairs, stuck my head under the tap and ungratefully flattened out the abominable quiffed loaf and combed it all forward into the critical style of the new day – the look of The Beatles. So not only were they breaking up the sounds of our house – the gramophone became the property of my sister and me, and with that its change of name to a record-player – but they also influenced the very look of a group of young Belfast lads who were just about entering their teenage years and leaving all that belonged to the fifties a long way behind them. Or so it seemed at the time.

As the journalist John Harris noted in a review of Mark Lewisohn's magisterial *The Beatles – All These Years* (Vol. 1): 'There are many of us, forever fascinated by the story, who still cannot quite fathom how the band managed to make music so endlessly full of interest, while also embodying the idea that as the world was changing at an unprecedented rate, they were always ahead of everyone else.' The music of how that transition happened is inscribed in the playful self-questioning of love, loyalty and loss that works its way into the language and refrains of *Rubber Soul*, not that we *knew* that then of course.

Indeed, I have to be careful here and not overburden the fourteen songs that make up *Rubber Soul* with too much of the know-how and intellectual machinery that came my way in the decades since we sat in those front rooms of numerous red-brick houses of upper north Belfast, with the music escaping out across the rain-swept genteel avenues or during languid summers before the curtain dropped on the kind of freedom we had enjoyed. Like our contemporaries throughout Britain and Ireland with whom we shared record magazines, BBC and ATV and the ground-breaking Radio Luxemburg and Radio Caroline, we were tuned into a new wave, even though The Beatles by 1965 were seen by some as the management. Other more unorthodox bands, such as The Small Faces, The Yardbirds, The Animals, briefly, Them, and of course the increasingly provocative presence of Bob Dylan, were considered as the true upholders of the faith. However, listening to them all never seemed to halt anyone's growth. I know I did, along with my mates. Belfast was like a listening post on blues music too, and we duly obliged, thrilled by Lightning Hopkins and all the black musicians who came our way, as well as the urban blues bands of John Mayall and Paul Butterfield. But how could you not 'dig' the likes of 'I'm Looking Through You', such a great song of longing and complaint which mixes local idiom with such ease?

And the idea of The Beatles consciously thinking about the language of their own place and time isn't entirely fanciful. Listening to *Rubber Soul* again, it struck me just how often reference is made in the lyrics to 'words'. Without straining too much for thematic coherence or an overriding 'meaning' to the album, it is true to say that *Rubber Soul* – from the playfulness of the title ('soul'/ 'sole'; real soul, plastic soul, imitative soul: the battling business in popular culture over authenticity) to the slightly distorted (and disturbed) cover image where only John is looking at the auditor through the goldfish bowl as the others gaze out of perspective – that this is a collection of lyrics which asks questions about communication and about how things seem to be:

> You don't look different
> But you have changed [...]
>
> Your lips are moving
> I cannot hear [...]
>
> You were above me
> But not today
> ('I'm Looking Through You')

The words 'aren't clear'; we hear, 'I've learned the game' – 'You're not the same.' But what does stay the same when, as these young men were learning very fast, their own lives were changing for ever right then and at a rapid pace. According to the album's liner notes: 'While making *Rubber Soul* [The Beatles] spent even more time perfecting their songs and when this was combined with a pressing deadline for completion of the LP, sessions often stretched into the early hours of the morning.' A hundred hours were spent in the studio between October and November 1965 and the last recording session lasted from 6 p.m. in the evening to 7 a.m. the following morning; along with *Rubber Soul*'s recording, 'Day Tripper' and 'We Can Work It Out' were also recorded and released. No wonder 'nowhere' crops up in the songs a couple of times because in a sense that's where they were heading as individuals – on the road, endlessly bustling from place to place, hotel to hotel, trying to keep their feet on the ground, performing before the camera constantly during interviews, photo-shoots – while everything and everyone around them was beginning to dance to a different tune:

> It's been a long time, now I'm coming
>   back home [...]

> I feel as though you ought to know
> That I've been good, as good as I can be
> ('Wait')

But was 'there anybody going to *listen*'? ('Girl') And what about 'trust'? 'Fame' too is more than just a word as it becomes more of a way of life with which the four lads have to cope and even to begin to question:

> Was she told when she was young
> That fame would lead to pleasure?
> Did she understand it when they said
> That a man must break his back
> To earn his day of leisure?
> ('Girl')

The male chauvinism here was part of the period, I guess we can say – part of the industrial vernacular that underpins other pulses in the lyrics. Although who today would get away with the opening lines of 'Run for Your Life': 'I'd rather see you dead, little girl / Than to be with another man'? The questions proliferate in *Rubber Soul*, of that there is no doubt; from 'What Goes On?' –

I used to think of nobody else
But you were just the same
You didn't even think of me
As someone with a name

– to 'The Word' with its echo of street religion tracts and 'Have you heard the word is love?' From '[i]n the good and the bad books that I have read' to 'words that go together well' ('Michelle') and 'a word or two' on George's 'Think for Yourself', *Rubber Soul* reads as a collection of highly *word*-conscious lyrics. How many pop songs use words like 'opaque' and 'rectify', for instance, nestled within the more customary form of address of forlorn love:

I left you far behind
The ruins of the life that you had in mind
And though you still can't see
I know your mind's made up,
You're gonna cause more misery
('Think for Yourself')

This plaintive, questioning, uncertain voice recurs throughout *Rubber Soul* – of not being able to explain, of losing contact and understanding, of parting and seeing things differently, from a separated distance:

I won't want to stay
I don't have much to say [...]

> Time after time
> You refuse to even listen
> ('You Won't See Me')

This is pitch-perfect domestic dialogue recalibrated as song – natural, direct, realistic speech patterns not dissimilar to the achievement of some of the novelists of the period, such as David Storey, Nell Dunn and John Braine, but with a deft, lighter touch. The difference is, of course, the medium that alters around the ironic points of the song:

> Baby, you can drive my car,
> And maybe I'll love you –
> *Beep-beep, mm, beep-beep, yeah*

They must have had some fun with 'Drive My Car'. Is it the case then, as Philip Norman states in his life of John Lennon, that at least seven of the songs in *Rubber Soul* were 'of an order so different, so vastly superior, it was hard to believe they sprang from the same musicians, the same studio or moment in time'? He continues:

> In them, John's and Paul's individual creative voices first come clearly into counterpoint: one that of a matchlessly artful, perfectly focused commercial songwriter, the other torn between the impulses of a poet, journalist, autobiographer, satirist, sloganeer, nostalgic and melancholic.

Certainly 'Nowhere Man', 'Norwegian Wood' and 'In My Life' carry the strange unpredictable edginess of poetry in a way that most of the other songs do not. While 'Michelle', both in words and music, has a classical simplicity of feeling expressed that it really is in a class all by itself.

But it is the way 'Norwegian Wood' catches the listener off guard that recalls the manner, first time around, of a Philip Larkin poem.

> I sat on a rug biding my time
> Drinking her wine
> We talked until two and then she said
> 'It's time for bed'
> ('Norwegian Wood')

The reference to Larkin may not be as far-fetched as it sounds, bearing in mind that Larkin's poem 'Annus Mirabilis', though written in 1967, is set a little earlier, with its celebrated tribute of refrain:

> Sexual intercourse began
> In nineteen sixty-three
> (Which was rather late for me) –
> Between the end of the *Chatterley* ban
> And the Beatles first LP.

But I can't seem to stray too far away from the overarching motif of *Rubber Soul*. While enigmas will always, rightly, remain about who the 'you' figures variously are in each of the lyrics, there is an underlying theme in the album that is conveyed most clearly, indeed starkly, in the simple (though far from simplistic) timbre of the vocals and words of 'In My Life'.

It is a great song of the sixties, marking the personal, yet representative, shift in John Lennon's moving away from his Liverpudlian background, upbringing, and all that he knew and felt for in that time and place. If it is a song of sentiment, so be it, but I can't say it is sentimental, or exploitative of the feelings he, along with the other Beatles, must have been wrestling with as fame and work was starting to separate them from their own most recent past – a theme that pervades so much of the writing of the time, including the poetry of Leeds-born Tony Harrison. Philip Norman provides useful background in his biography of John Lennon:

> [Lennon] sketched out a song that would use poetic observation in the style of Wordsworth or Tennyson, recalling the Liverpool he had known as a child and lamenting how, even over his short lifetime, that old, solid world of ships and docks had all but vanished. The choice of subject can have been no accident. His Aunt Mimi was soon to leave Mendips for Harbour View, finally closing the long-extended chapter of his boyhood. His original lyric was a wistful return to

years gone by, reliving the bus journey he had taken countless times from Menlove Avenue into central Liverpool, via Penny Lane, Church Road, the Dutch and St Columbus, and the Dockers' Umbrella [elevated railway] that they pulled down. Somehow, this first attempt to immortalise Penny Lane refused to gel, so John cut the 'travelogue' part of the song, making it instead a personal requiem for 'friends and lovers ... people and things that went before'. Even with an 'I love you' payoff, it broke new ground.

In the onward-and-upward-thrusting mid-sixties, nostalgia was still comparatively rare. A 25-year-old pop superstar was the least likely person to be looking back over his life as if time were already growing short:

All these places have their moments
With lovers and friends I still can recall
Some are dead and some are living
In my life, I've loved them all
('In My Life')

'In My Life' is a kind of poem of farewell as 'memories lose their meaning' and become instead songs, just as *Rubber Soul* would mark the threshold behind which The Beatles of *Help!* were moving on to the more challenging moods and musical experiments of *Revolver* and *Sgt. Pepper's*.

'The Beatles', Stewart Parker wrote, in only his second column for the *Irish Times* in May 1970, 'formed in 1960 and now they seem to have split in 1970. It's as if they instinctively felt that their corporate identity belonged solely to the decade in which they revolutionised popular music, and to which they virtually contributed a style of life. But maybe the split is only temporary; or maybe, against all the odds, Lennon and McCartney will each develop in unprecedented ways to surpass their former combined brilliance.' Parker's words sum it all up, the 'combined brilliance' that outlived the decade of its making and survives as fresh and undaunted as the day it was first made and heard half a century ago.

TWO

Robert Lowell and his poetry are indelibly associated
in my mind with one place – Bangor, the County Down
town on the southern shores of Belfast Lough. Though
I didn't realise it at the time when I started to read him
in the late 1960s and early 1970s, his New England
villages and communities were being channelled in my
mind through that coastline of Helen's Bay, Ballyholme
Esplanade, Groomsport, Ballymacormick Point and
the Copeland islands. The trawlers berthed in the
little harbour in Bangor – now an extended marina –
carried distant family resemblances in 'Water':

> Remember? We sat on a slab of rock.
> From this distance in time,
> it seems the color
> of iris, rotting and turning purpler,
>
> but it was only
> the usual gray rock
> turning the usual green
> when drenched by the sea.

There was also the wry, sardonic modern twist of
Lowell's 'English' that found a deep echo in the young

private lives we were living then, spreading our wings in north Belfast and picking out from the school anthologies the new poetry of Americans like Lowell and those who, at one point or another, had come under his influence, such as Sylvia Plath. Donald Hall's third edition of Michael Roberts's ground-breaking anthology, *The Faber Book of Modern Verse*, was the set text for 'A' level and from that book the Americans emerged supreme, catching a mood of exhilaration that spread out from the American late fifties into the transatlantic sixties, bringing great music in its wake but also the anxieties and challenges of Vietnam and the nuclear arms race:

> Burnished, burned-out, still burning as
>   the year
> you lead me to our stamping ground.
> The city and its cruising cars surround
> the Public Garden. All's alive [.]
> ('The Public Garden', *For the Union
>   Dead*)

But it wasn't solely this supercharged and hip modernity which Lowell caught as the mood of the moment. Reading Lowell also provoked a certain kind of local resonance, a complex and unexplicated sense of the puritan inheritances of Northern Protestantism; a familial feeling that pervades *Life Studies*, *For the Union Dead* and *Near the Ocean*. I certainly would have been barely conscious of this at the time but the social proprieties Lowell anatomises in '91 Revere Street' and picks out with such chastening detail elsewhere in *Life Studies*, in his portraits of his mother, father, grandfather and others, carried a marked similarity to the anecdotes and handed-down family stories of the delayed post-war world I had known in the drawing rooms and front rooms of ancient aunts whose only love had perished in one of the world wars:

> Born ten years and yet an aeon
> too early for the twenties,
> Mother, you smile
> as if you saw your Father
> inches away yet hidden, as when he
>   groused behind a screen
> over a National Geographic Magazine
> whenever young men came to court you
> back in those settled years of World War
>   One.
> ('During Fever')

And of course for any young boy or girl growing out of adolescence into that Northern industrial society with its 'suburban factories' at the very heart of its major city, the contrasting civic landscape of Lowell's statues in 'New England greens' might also have found a strong local resonance. Firstly, in the very sense of commemoration with the public display and ongoing rites of marking the state's identification with the sacrifice of two world wars:

> The stone statues of the abstract Union
>   Soldier
> grow slimmer and younger each year –
> wasp-wasted, they doze over musket
> and muse through their sideburns...
> ('For the Union Dead')

Church cenotaphs, military monuments, regimental flags, this was the very stuff of our immediate lives which Lowell strangely helped us to see. But he also prompted in his poems a critical edge which opened up the background of social life and urged his readers to see another story, the *actual* society:

> When I crouch to my television set,
> The drained faces of Negro school-
>   children rise like balloons.
> ('For the Union Dead')

By the time *For the Union Dead* was published in Britain in 1965, Northern Irish society was on the edge of its own political turmoil, which would lead into civil unrest and, eventually, widespread violence:

> I swim like a minnow
> Behind my studio window.
>
> Our end drifts nearer,
> The moon lifts,
> radiant with terror.
> The state

is a diver under a glass bell.
('Fall 1961')

Lowell's crucial example could show how it was possible to have a poetic response to a political situation. But also, he revealed how a society can contain inside itself contradictory cultural pulses and ideological pressures, stability, conventions, ways of life which seem unchanging but are actually on the point of transition, sometimes radical transition.

There was much in those early books that passed me by. As with songs of the time, the 'boardwalks' and 'sidewalks', 'levees' and 'Chevy's', the argot of consumerist and vernacular America was repeated but without my really knowing what it was all about; except for the provocatively individualistic urban energy that contained a shadowing, shriving sense of uncertainty:

> Everything had been swept bare,
> furnished, garnished and aired.
>
> Everything's changed for the best –
> how quivering and fierce we were,
> there snowbound together
> simmering like wasps
> in our tent of books!
> ('The Old Flame')

Simmering 'like wasps' remains as stunning as the 'two cops on horseback' who 'clop through the

April rain' in 'The Drinker', checking 'the parking meter violations', 'their oilskins yellow as forsythia'. *Forsythia?* Marrying these local details to the 'man ... killing time', the Herzog-like cheese that 'wilts in the rat-trap, / the milk turns to junket in the cornflakes bowl' and the Melvillean ancestral images of 'the whale's warm-hearted blubber, foundering down / leagues of ocean, gasping whiteness', was/is simply reality-changing; the kind of electric stuff that knocked a young reader (and his much older self) into a reverie of desire. 'I want to write like that', but then reality checks in. So back to Bangor.

For many thousands of Belfast families, Bangor represented the summer. It was to Bangor during the fifties that we went for a month's holiday, renting a house in which lived my mother, sister, grandmother, and which several of their friends visited from time to time. Occasionally my uncle and his pal dropped by, but outside of some time spent on the beach at Ballyholme, their minds were fixed on the bars and dancehalls. A taxi took us to the North Eastern station. The train journey from Belfast to Bangor was a ceremonial affair of expectation that was only ever complete by entering the station in Bangor, stepping into Main Street and looking down towards the McKee clock tower, the mine and the rattling chains of coal buckets or the spinning wheel of the little fair.

We stayed in comfortable red-brick houses with tidy gardens and small backyards. The houses were full of heavy furniture and carpets, stairways and cubby-holes, shadowy back bedrooms and craft-worked etchings of the Mourne Mountains, Helen's Bay or some well-known 'place of interest' like the Mull of Kintyre or Portpatrick. The few books around were miscellanies; Saturday Bedside anthologies. The hearths were covered by fire screens and tables of one sort or another popped up out of corners, at bay windows, between doors.

We had connections in Bangor, friends of my grandmother's. One had a shop in Main Street and we went there for tea, enviously eyeing their son, a tanned and athletic young man who worked his summers on the pleasure boats. Another friend of my grandmother's, whom I was intrigued by with her quiet manner and marvellous 'country' accent, lived in Prospect Road and had fostered our dog when we moved house from suburban Belfast to one of the busier arterial roads on the city's north side. She and her sister passed 'snaps' of men and women I knew nothing about between themselves and wistfully smiled. We went from their house into Ward Park to look at the big gun, flowerbeds, and bowling green, and then took in the last of the evening sun. There was something hurt about the sisters.

From time to time my grandmother's Belfast friends dropped in on day visits or even stayed a night or two by way of offering her diversion. Their 'real' holidays were spent in the Isle of Man or Bournemouth and she also went to visit her sister in London. I fell in love with one of those friends at the age of six or seven.

She had flaming red hair and adoring eyes and smoked 'plain' cigarettes.

On deck-chairs we would sit facing the sea. The ice cream shop on the promenade was like a little bunker and up above it stood tall silent guest houses. Most afternoons beyond at Pickie Pool, and throughout Sundays, songs were sung and although we never took part, we would listen and move on:

> Each little flower that opens,
> Each little bird that sings,
> He made their glowing colours,
> He made their tiny wings:
>
> The purple-headed mountain,
> The river running by,
> The sunset and the morning,
> That brightens up the sky.
> (Mrs C.F. Alexander: 1818–1895)

There's always somewhere that holds a special place in one's memory of childhood and growing up. Lowell's poems are filled with such recollections of times and New England places he grew up in and revisited from his Boston base. A place that is set in the backroom of the mind with its landscape and sound and smells and a kind of elusive reality. For many Belfast people, Bangor fulfilled that elsewhere life. Bangor provided an intimate and alluring hold on generations of ordinary people long before the cheap flights sent them off in every global direction imaginable.

For the sixties' generation, Bangor provided a summer of day-trip possibility – dancing, meeting girls, hanging out on the sea front, being cool at the 'seaside'. We hitched there. And for a couple of summers we stayed there overnight, in a friend's family chalet-cum-bungalow, played our music. For those who went before us – like those in the 1940s awaiting the D-Day embarkation to liberate Europe, or before that, in the hazier days of the thirties between the wars – the place seemed to stay unchanged and unchangeable.

When I think of Bangor today, it is through the viewfinder of both a late sixties' pleasure ground, but also that of a very young lad going down with his own family on holiday in the fifties, staying in rented houses off Dufferin Avenue. Or a little later as a boy scout on an endurance test, pitching up in the Clandeboye estate and rising in the dewy morning to the sound of cattle breathing over our tiny tent.

Bangor was also a home-from-home for my late mother and stepfather, their last harbour in the new century. Walking along Ballyholme, strolling up above Pickie Pool, sitting down in Ward Park, looking across to the tall houses of Prospect Road where those grand 'aunts' had moved to from post-war Belfast, Bangor really was an imagined neighbourhood as much as a real place. But throughout it all, Bangor wasn't associated in my mind at least with cultural history or with the ecclesiastical tradition such as it actually held. Not at all. And even less did I know then about the direct links between Bangor and the Dufferins (the local landed family) who included Caroline Blackwood, a valuable writer and Lowell's third wife. Ignorance blossomed in the mood music of my time. Beside the bedside annuals of the fifties there was Riesling and Bob Dylan in the sixties. It was also about leaving on trains and buses home to a dusky north Belfast when it was already lighting-up time and the inevitable question arose about when next we'd head back down.

All along that coast, there is the magic and mystery of where the land meets the sea. People foregathered where their spiritual guides had established monasteries since 555. The inducements and energies of life there remain strong and empowering. I can still feel the mood take hold of excitement when I recall stepping out of the railway station and look down Main Street to imagine the coal boats clanking, hear the gulls cry. As in the poem 'Returning' with its 'sheltered little resort, / where the members of my gang / are bald-headed, in business', Lowell provides no wriggle room for the nostalgia of self-deceit. This might well be one of his greatest poetic legacies for a time such as today that praises easy sentiment and the imperative of instant response:

> Yet sometimes I catch my vague mind
> circling with a glazed eye
> for a name without a face, or a face
>   without a name,

and at every step,
I startle them. They start up,
dog-eared, bald as baby birds.

When Lowell goes further back to the Sunday dinners he endured as a small boy in Revere Street, Boston, we can identify the sense of anxiety and the strain of the young boy seeking, through the older poet's recollection, 'out'. As he recalibrates his father's delayed life in the wonderful memoir in *Life Studies*, there is a powerful feeling that Lowell's manic energy was born, first and foremost, of frustration with 'waiting for the new life' he wanted to grab with both hands for himself:

> Perhaps I exaggerate their embarrassment because they hover so grayly in recollection and seem to anticipate ominously my father's downhill progress as a civilian and Bostonian. It was to be expected, I suppose, that Father should be in irons for a year or two, while becoming detached from his old comrades and interests, while waiting for the new life.
> ('91 Revere Street')

In 1969 I sat my 'A' levels and wrote on poetry in the English examination. I had read Al Alvarez's *The New Poetry*, which further underlined the opening-up of the 'English' canon to American poets – as those contemporary American poets included in *The Faber Book of Modern Verse* reappeared. In May the following year I was invited to a dress dance at Belfast's Queen's University. A friend's girlfriend wanted me to go on a blind date with *her* friend. So off the four of us went – me the younger in dress suit, swallowing Bushmills whiskey; and a friendship bloomed. I would meet the girl, and we would attend classical music recitals in the Ulster Hall. In that brief time we spent together, barely a summer, she quoted Robert Lowell and from the house she shared with her family in Bangor, produced his books, including a hardback of *Near the Ocean*. I heard in that contemporary ironic voice nuances and inflections close to those I knew but had not really *heard* before as poetry, certainly in the Belfast out of which I was growing increasingly more impatient to be gone.

While I had been reading a lot and trying to assimilate all this work into some kind of coherence, I can see now that it was the figure of Robert Lowell whose poetry had made, from that early age, such a deep impression on me, and proved both creatively troublesome to take in and also exhilarating. And when I look at my own efforts since the early 1970s, it is clear that Lowell goes very much deeper than I'd previously thought. The division between past and present, and the *violent* sundering of that continuity out of which one's cultural identity, memory and tradition emerges, alongside the developing of an individual voice, led me to the blunt, almost physical, realisation that there is an inevitability about change;

it is simply the principle by which we make life valuable and renewing. Robert Lowell taught that lesson both in personal but more significantly in social and political terms through those poems of his which were simply unflinchingly of their time.

GREAT VICTORIA STREET
BAPTIST CHURCH

THREE

My maternal great-grandfather was an Orangeman. The story goes that there would have been a banner dedicated to him but his family demurred. I never met William. He was of Huguenot stock, married a woman of another refugee stock and fitted into Belfast life as a man of his turn-of-the-last-century times. Growing up in north Belfast, I was fascinated by him. His name was still known around and about and that intrigued me as mementoes of his life were still kept in the house; I was particularly interested by one that I have to this day. It is a newspaper cartoon, which shows him, a pair of britches in hand, an old-fashioned, unadorned sash over his shoulder, tearing across cobblestones under the slogan DUTY CALLS! When I was a kid, I hadn't a clue what that duty meant and it was just as well that William was well gone because we would have rowed the bit out over his patriarchal unionism.

Throughout the late 1950s I was taken to watch the Twelfth of July parades. We would stand outside the City Hall, our backs up against the ropes, and wait for the carriages to arrive, within which the grandees of the different orders stood, and there would be a kind of embarrassed banter as the preacher, with his doomful black sandwich-board proverb strapped to his chest, raising his heavy Bible up in the air and stamping his foot, called vengeance or foreboding upon us all. Were we *sinners*?

Behind, the kiss-me-quick hat brigade linked arms and danced; jolly little women with Union Jack skirts, aprons and bowler hats, like butchers, waved umbrellas, and the bands streamed by, wedged between them, serried ranks of men, waving, pointing their sons towards mothers, wives, brothers with infants on their shoulders, and the music cascaded down Royal Avenue and veered right and left again and on down the Dublin Road. 'Kilty' bands, military bands, flute bands, bands from Scotland which were called hucky-mucky, men with shining white gloves, sabres, little trays with icons placed on them, banners of all marvellous silks with images of queens, kings, stern men, martial figures, historical settings; and sometimes there would be a delay in the procession, and a band would stop in front of you and you could watch the bandsmen and their leader walking around them and the banners would sway some more and the young boys who held the black or white or orange strings would twirl them in their hands, or the big drummer would have someone hitch up the drum for a brief rest, although I never saw a Lambeg drum then; never in all my life.

We did not go to the field. Sometimes we'd return after tea to see the men come back though. But by the mid-sixties that had stopped. Something was creeping in which seemed different from before. Then we stopped going altogether. I don't know why. All I remember is the Eleventh Night and the flames bursting up into the sky in the Brickies behind our home; and in the morning the drum-roll as a banner was unfurled in the Grand Master's back garden in a house I could see from my back window. Tea was served and then the lodge joined up with its band and they made their way along Jellico Avenue and Alexandra Park onto the Antrim Road towards Clifton Street and the beginning of the Belfast procession.

Many years later, when all this ceremony was known worldwide as standing for only one thing – a triumphalist bazaar – I wrote a sequence of very short poems about growing up in north Belfast called simply, 'Six Scenes':

> The Past Master's
> taut face gleams
> like the windows
> of his makeshift
> glasshouse.
> The teacup shakes
> from stiff gloves
> he has on as
> the banner unfurls
> to a swaying scene
> of Slave and Queen.

It would take a great film director like Antonioni to capture the unbelievable clash of pomp, propriety, machismo, bigotry and pride that went into those Twelfth celebrations in the fifties and early sixties.

They were street-theatre before the term was invented; like Corpus Christi without Christ. What these parades meant, or were made to mean to the rest of civic society – the unbelievers, if you like – is part of the story that leads directly into the crisis of democracy there. I know it took me about seven years to unshackle myself from all the tragedy and confusions of the seventies that had gathered throughout the early years of the Troubles into a very dark time and one that I had tried to express in a very constrained volume of poems, my first, *Sheltering Places* (1978). The intervening years were all about relocating and seeing, literally, where and what I had come from – a typically Belfast Protestant hybrid of refugee and planter stock, with profound stability and instability masked under the surface of generations of adapting to and ordering that provincial Northern society.

My great-grandfather lived most of his life on the Duncairn Gardens and, though he was dead before I arrived, his influence was very strong through his daughter, Ethel, my grandmother, with whom I lived. 'Billy' Chartres worked for the *Belfast Telegraph* and *Ireland Saturday Night*. He was a staunch unionist and a leading member of the Orange Order of his day, and was an obsessive football man, having helped set up the Junior League. As a journalist, he wrote under the name 'The Wanderer' – which might have something to do deep down with his own family's spiritual roots as refugees at one time, or it may not.

Anyway, it took a long time to sort out what this invisible man meant to me. Although, as I say,

I never met him, he lived in my mind and through photographs, press cuttings, cartoons and family reminiscences; it took me ages to realise that William Bailey Chartres represented the past. He it was who dramatised the history of my immediate surroundings; he was the tradition that I could have followed having thought about accepting a job as a 'cub' reporter on the *Belfast Telegraph* in the late sixties. When I left Belfast, he travelled with me, like a shade. I had endless imaginary encounters with Billy Chartres rebuking and chastising me, and ending up like Alfred Hitchcock walking through my poems when he got half a chance. His was an instructive presence I couldn't easily shake off.

Often critics and journalists talk about 'Northern Protestants' as if they were dour, narrow, bigoted, unimaginative, mean, spiteful and so on. I am sure many are: as many as there are in any community in any place in the world. I get seriously fed up, though, with the way ordinary Protestants are represented as *cultureless*. It's when I think of William Bailey Chartres and the family he came from and the one that came from him, which includes my friends, and me, and their families whom I knew growing up in Belfast. Whatever about their faults ('our' faults), I do not see them the way they are often portrayed. It shouldn't be too arduous a task to show the intellectual, cultural, musical, philosophical and artistic traditions that lie beneath the stereotypical images with which Northern Protestants are all too often imprisoned.

Be that as it may, it took me a long time to understand that Billy Chartres was, in fact, *my* past and I had better try and understand it (and him) rather than run away. Indeed, it took the years from 1978 to 1985 living in Galway, starting a family, finding work, experiencing life there, travelling back and forth to Belfast, trying to explain what was going on, before Billy Chartres and I came to terms with each other. He challenged me and I responded as best I could with a clutch of poems that eventually found their way into a collection of poems, *The Lundys Letter* (1985). The Old Testament, the legacy of British military history, the customs and attitudes and experiences and desires of all the people I had grown up with found their way into both that collection and the one that followed, *Sunday School* (1991).

My belief is that poets are poets first and citizens second. No matter what the religion, gender or race, poetry is the thing that matters. When people, be they politicians or professional commentators, proclaim that poets *should* write about this or that, that the poet *must* identify with this community or that – you had better watch out, because we are no longer talking about art but about propaganda. Poetry, like music, or dance, or painting, or sport for that matter, thrives when it is given its own space and hasn't some well-meaning, or not so well-meaning, guru breathing down your neck. My poems are addressed to whomsoever has the chance and cares to listen. I think of them in terms of Herman Melville's comment in *Moby-Dick*: 'All these things are not without their meaning.'

I hate stereotypes and the one-upmanship and jockeying for position between different groups as if 'culture' could ever belong to one side to the disadvantage of the other. The basic truth about culture and art is that it cannot be segregated or worn like a badge of identity. It becomes something else then; a slogan, a form of superiority. I dislike all the tired, stale old arguments about *this* sense of identity being more natural, or historically more valid than *that*, as if there was some hierarchy in which we are formed or which we have to possess to make us 'great' or, at least, greater than the other. Writing poems, finding the language, the forms and the voice, is difficult enough.

From an emigrant background, with a relatively young and inexperienced widowed mother and a younger brother to look after, living in Belfast in the closing decades of the nineteenth and early decades of the twentieth century, it couldn't have been easy for Billy Chartres. He worked hard and prospered, and his daughters – my Belfast grandmother and my London great-aunt – seemed well set up for life. After I wrote a couple of poems about this man, he disappeared. As one door closed, another opened. Following the strange tales of family names like any genealogical root-searcher, I discovered that the woman the Huguenot Chartres had married was called Mary Jane Quartz.

Both had met in north Belfast, in a district of mixed religious and ethnic origins, the kind of district that seemingly did not exist in the north of Ireland, never mind Belfast. I dare say they buried their distinct histories in order to get on as best they could; a not uncommon strategy for emigrants, or the children of emigrants. Mary's story, my great-grandmother's story, needed its own commemoration. She became a subversive presence, a sociable, physical figure who handed on both the sociability and uncertainty of her own unconventional heritage, waddling down Royal Avenue in the middle of the road, stopping traffic, carrying a money belt under the ample skirts, looking (one suspects) for a life beyond the seemingly leaden class-conscious proprieties of her husband and the time.

The poem 'Quartz' tells a familiar emigrant story, apocryphal in part, about the journey of a generation of Europeans towards the end of the nineteenth century, duped by unscrupulous shipping companies or sea captains. It moves from the austerity and masculinity of the patriarchal order, which had defined for almost two centuries the public face of Belfast, to *her* Belfast, and the vulnerable hope, in the midst of real personal challenge, of similarly courageous women making a life for themselves and their families, wherever and however they could. Without laying too much freight on the slight shoulders of the poem, 'Quartz' meant for me an imaginative movement away from history to a personal voice, from power play to a yearning to live, imagining a different kind of cultural reality by actually inhabiting none, albeit with that dash of the apocryphal. Maybe from these hidden, un-canonical sources a deeper sense of a common culture

will surface in twenty-first-century Northern Ireland,
indeed throughout the country as a whole, and that
these differences of background will be celebrated in
future rather than locked away as idiosyncratic bit-
parts in the big picture:

> Quartz
> *for Katrina Goldstone*
>
> So there is something I want to know,
> great-grandmother, reclining on
>   whichever
> foreign shore or ambrosial meadow,
> taking a second look at the old place –
>
> the valiant village, the provincial district,
> the back-breaking hill-climb to the
>   apartment,
> the quiet evening square in this country
>   town
> or that frontier post, down by the coastal
>   resort
>
> of some famous lake, say, with Roman
>   baths,
> or a minority language – I want to know
> who your grand dame was, or
>   paterfamilias,
> disembarking in a draughty shed,
>   thinking

Liverpool or Belfast was really New
  York,
blinking in the greyish light of a noisy
  dawn,
looking out for rooming
  houses, a decent hotel,
putting one foot in front of the other,

taking the first right and walking,
  walking,
past the shipping offices and custom
  houses,
the rattling trams and carters and mill
  girls,
the steep factories and squat churches till
  the hills

converge upon this three-storied terrace
with the curtains drawn, the bell-pull
  shining,
and you pull the bell-pull and in
  whatever
English you'd learned you stepped in.

FOUR

In the 1950s, London was our second home. Half our family had emigrated to the British capital early on in the century and there was a regular jockeying back and forth from London where my great-aunt and her extended family lived.

Over the years, we travelled by boat and train and eventually by air. We attended weddings and funerals, holidayed there, and I lived there for a little while before opting for Belfast in the late 1960s.

We were Belfast Protestants, but not of the churchy or party-political type; Britain existed as England. It was the cyclorama to our lives. We listened to BBC on the radio, and watched BBC and ITV when the time came. Our house retained the blackout blinds from World War II up to the late 1950s. The bottled sauces and Indian tea, Camp Coffee and medicines, brand-named jumpers and socks, Tate and Lyle's Golden Syrup with its sleeping lion and sleepier slogan, Christmas cake and boxes of biscuits were all British Made; my toys, too, and comics and footballs.

When it came to school, our history was British and the songs (along with accompanying gestures), which the slightly electric Miss Gray taught us, were English and Scottish ballads:

> My body lies over the ocean
> My body lies over the sea
> My body lies over the ocean
> O bring back my body to me.

The fact that it was *bonnie* seems to have passed us by. And the headmaster of my primary school, the mythopoetically named Mr Nelson, reputed to have looked exactly the same when my uncle attended the school, a generation earlier, walked about with a raffish stoop and had, in his small unlit office, two memorable symbols: a fighter plane on a perspex mantle, and a globe of the world demarcating the Empire. He was a proud, dignified and tolerant man, so far as we could tell, and he never interfered in our lives. On the other hand, the teacher who looked like Clark Gable, spoke with a distinct twang under the voluptuous moustache, and smoked Senior Service, bore all the marks of a devil-may-care veteran.

The war was the centrepiece in our upbringing. Its effect on the Belfast of my boyhood was clear. Behind our house, the Brickies – a derelict site; above us, the deserted US Army installation – a warren of outhouses and garages; away below us, 'prefabs' which housed hundreds of families whose homes had been destroyed when Belfast was blitzed in 1941.

And the stories of my great-grandmother sitting through the Blitz under the stairs, giving out to the

Jerries as an unexploded bomb lodged in the back wall; my grandmother working in an ammunitions factory, ducking IRA bullets; my mother's romance with a touring Army bandsman; the men you could see and hear throughout the fifties and sixties, on the buses late at night, or stumbling home of an evening, regimental blazers and grey flannels, talking away to themselves or to their indignant yet knowing wives.

Football was the other big influence in those early years. Before the break-up of their marriage, my father – the touring Army bandsman – took me to Solitude, the Cliftonville ground, home to the Reds, amateurs as they were then in the early 1950s. A little later, when we moved to Skegoneill, my bedroom overlooked Brantwood, a small pitch that figured large in our lives. It had a spooky deserted house on its left flank, the southern bank of the ground was sufficiently raised so that you could look down over lower north Belfast and way beyond, and the sweeping pleasure-lands of The Grove, where I spent most of my boyhood evenings, ran to its easterly walls. A friend was the mascot of Brantwood, as a result of which we attended the entire home 'fixtures' with semi-official status.

I played left back, and occasionally the slightly more glamorous left half, for primary school and boy-scouts but didn't really make the grade in the highly charged devotion to 'soccer' at secondary school. By then I had switched allegiance and attended Seaview on the Shore Road, the gallant home stadium of The Hatchetmen, Crusaders, nestling along the foreshore of the lough and the North Eastern Railway:

45

Bimbo Weatherup
hammers one in;
the crowd goes daft;
a train shoots past.
On the hill
in front of us
the houses stretch up
like a ladder from
the Shore to Antrim Road.
In-between is where we are,
backs to the sea.
('Six Scenes')

Linfield, or the Blues, the pan-Belfast club based at Windsor, had a ferocious reputation and when they travelled to the Shore Road there was a sense of an army on the move. Crossing town every day to school on the east side brought me into the 'Glens' territory (Glentoran) and the swinging army-surplus satchels of Glens-obsessed supporters. Those were passionate times in which the slightly Anglicised voice of Captain Danny Blanchflower ('ore play-eers') cut a dignified swathe through the fucking and blinding that went on back home in the swaying terraces of men and boys. The white immaculate v-neck of his Tottenham jersey said it all: he was our better half; our white knight. It was Derek ('Deek') Duggan (Wolves), a towering unconquerable one-of-the-lads, behind whose shadow would wistfully and shyly emerge the artist in us all, George Best. When Kenneth Wolstenholme spoke his name on 'Match of the Day' on Saturday nights, Best had become a real star, a shooting star.

Belfast was synonymous with football. Whatever psychic clock we worked to, changing games by season without any announcement or instruction, from conkers, 'marlies' and a particularly painful hand-game using lollipop-sticks, to street-games whose names I cannot recall, football was the air we breathed.

Hallways, monk's benches full of boots, yards, entries, back-gardens, parks, side-streets, pitches, jerseys, bedrooms bedecked with posters of teams and star-players (alongside the motorbikes and the few 'rock' bands), imitation league-tables, flags, pennants, arms tattooed, school-bags scrawled on, summers totally given over to talking and playing football, picking a team (and the gaminess and machismo of that), playing until night fell and you couldn't even see the ball. A famous newspaper competition was called 'Spot the Ball' – an act of pure imagination, if ever there was one. And the ball itself was a sodden, heavy, laced leather ball, 'a bladder'. Until the new plastic football came in and there was the machinery that went with keeping it inflated and the constant jockeying to and from the local shop, Billy Duddy's, to get the new footballs or better ones. And the reluctance to give all this up come September and the return to school when the professional season returned in England along with the local versions that ran from the top clubs to the rest around us, like Brantwood, Dungannon Swifts or Chimney Corner, and that ticker-tape on BBC Grandstand before the voice (what was his name?) gave the full results throughout the English and Scottish league tables: Stenhousemuir, Plymouth Argyle; such names with which to conjure on a dark Saturday night in the middle of February.

> The baize tablecloth is velvety with age,
> the tassels torn. You stretch on a sofa
> watching Tottenham Hotspur walk all
>   over Sheffield Wednesday.
> Whitewash on the backyard peels in
>   scales
> and the slack weeps in its makeshift shed.
> The rain drip-drops down gutters and
>   drains.
>
> Let there be another Ice Age, a God to
>   speak with Moses,
> the skies open up and rivers part –
> this is where a young man finds himself,
> at half-time making tea by the sink,
> below glass-panelled presses that give
>   back a look
> of the great-grandfather on his mother's
>   side.
> ('The Bright Hour: 1 Genesis')

By the mid-sixties all this had given way to music; the World Cup flared up like a spectacular piece of theatre, but the intensity had gone, along with the kind of life of that time. Years later I was back outside our old house recording a programme for local television about leaving and crossing borders. I suggested we go into the football ground that I used to look into from my bedroom window and beyond it towards the amber city lights of Belfast. As we approached, the crew and myself, the door opened and one of the groundsmen stepped out. Behind him, tethered on a rope, and totally unenamoured by our presence, stood a ram, his jagged horns twisting this way and that, and those shocking eyes. It was a bizarre, almost perverse image out of the classical world, as if we had trespassed upon some hallowed ground of the past and this detached, self-preoccupied custodial creature was there as a rebuke. 'Hey, mister', one the goat's minders shouted, 'would you take our photee?'

I bate a hasty retreat from the low walls, the hut of changing rooms, the slagging and counter-charges as men shouted at referees and each other; the straight-backed, Gladstone-collared club president, the summer carnival that set up shop every year, the kick and rush and smash as the bladder thudded into the top of the net and the two or three young lads peered through the dusk into the haunted house when the match ended.

One morning in 1965 I was sitting on the 64 Downview bus, heading into the city centre for school. It was raining and the bus was packed with people, most of whom were smoking cigarettes and looking out of the steamed-up windows. A strange thing happened. I looked around me and in a flash of histrionic insight realised, almost smugly, that, like the drunken Minister in the film *Zulu*, they would, *we* all would, some day die. No proverbs; no sandwich men; no ministers; no amount of praying, church-going or piety could get us around that simple fact of life.

A few years later, I read until I was almost blue in the face everything by Jean-Paul Sartre and Albert Camus and considered that my earlier experience had been what every good existentialist knows to be an encounter with the Absurd. If Roquentin, Meursault and Mathieu, leading figures in Sartre's fiction, were not exactly the best role-models for a Belfast Protestant teenager with a paltry attendance at Sunday school and church, who was supposed to know any the different? The irony is, I suppose, that the family I came from, while not being orthodox in their religion – anything but – did have a lot of time for spiritualism. Life-after-death was a fairly acceptable norm. Not things that go bump in the night, hovering tables and trumpets of ectoplasm like a week's washing, although there was one book with photographs of such things that had a faintly Faustian sense of transgression about it, and still has to this day. No, the spiritual dimension to my upbringing ran quietly but constitutionally contrary to the eyeballing of existence upon which Sartre insisted. But, like a dutiful disciple, I was hooked by his militant agnosticism. Roquentin remarks in *Nausea* (Penguin Modern Classics, June 1969, four shillings, Dali's

Triangular Hour on the cover): 'Most of the time, because of their failure to fasten on to words, my thoughts remain misty and nebulous. They assume vague, amusing shapes and are then swallowed up. I promptly forget them.' And the rallying call I underlined clearly held no truck at all with religion, spirituality or the likes of that. 'I want no secrets [Roquentin remarks], no spiritual condition, nothing ineffable; I am neither a virgin nor a priest, to play at having an inner life'. Why an 'inner life' should have been seen then as an almost derisory thing I cannot now recall. Yet, all the years which separate the underliner of that passage from the present writer has also seen, in Ireland as elsewhere, a great emphasis being put upon the public confession of one's innermost secrets and personal experience. In fact, confession has become not only a marketing tool but a lifestyle. A private life is not a life unless everything is exposed from the inside out.

In rejecting all this, the Duchamp portrait by Jacques Villon on the Penguin cover of *The Outsider* says it all: angular, haunting and uncompromising, it embodies a feeling of calm, benign, hard-won indifference. Resisting sham solution, self-indulgence, fashionable anger and privileged resentment, preoccupied instead with austere moderation and artistic reserve, it should come as no surprise that Camus offered an alternative, if allied, vision to that generally on offer in post-war, pre-Troubles Belfast. It is something Derek Mahon captures in his poem dedicated to Albert Camus, 'Death and the Sun':

> The interior dialogue of flesh and stone,
> his life and death a work of art
> conceived in the silence of the heart.

'Existentialism' was an aggressive way of bringing oneself up in a city coming down with religion and atrophied politics. It was a thing of the heart; iron in the soul:

> On everything I love, on the rust in the yards, on the rotten planks of the fence, a miserly, sensible light is falling, like the look you give, after a sleepless night, at the decisions you made enthusiastically the day before, at the pages you wrote straight off without a single correction.

What Roquentin writes in his diary was the real deal. Where the spiritualism came in is something else – a joker in the pack, the hazel wand that bewitches and divines 'truth' rather than discerning 'the reality of a situation'. This belief in an afterlife had a strong, palpable existence in the North of my childhood, possibly as a throwback from the mourning of two world wars, I don't know. But it is something without which the suffering there would have been even more unbearable for the bereaved. The testimony during the Troubles of so many in front rooms talking of their murdered loved ones bespeaks a faith in God, or in an after-life, that cannot be overlooked. So, I am less sure about religion. It has stanched many wounds, ritualised and dignified what is so grim in its very ordinariness – death. If institutionalised religion lacked sunlight, that probably tells us more about the North as a whole and about the role and legacy of its churches than it does about those who attended them.

FIVE

In memory of Joe Bradley

It was a choice between art history in England and English in Northern Ireland. Queen's in Belfast was too much like home and when a friend said he was going to (what was then called) the New University of Ulster, that was it. We headed off in his black Morris Minor one September morning in 1971 and moved into the same B&B for the first term. The house was run by a business-like woman who took good care of us and her house. Everything was in its place, put there with a kind of brisk love. Going to university was not the logical thing to do. Most of my friends either had not bothered or did not get the chance. We were, after all, children of the sixties, full of grace, and it took some time to settle into the troubled world that the seventies brought about. Anyway, Coleraine in 1971 was a compromise. The campus looked like an airport but, behind it, the Bann curved its way towards the coast and the magnificent sea – along the shoreline of which holiday resorts clung, full of three- and four-storied guest houses with great bay windows like puffed-out bellies – and a thin wind that would cut right through you.

It was not long before a few of us, mostly from Glasgow and Belfast, had banded together and joined the Labour Club. NUU's political birth had been uppermost in many minds but, accepting the fact it was there to stay, we sat in seminar rooms and discussed the 'Law of the Diminishing Returns of Profit' and held a radical stall outside the refectory every week. When things were looking bad, some of us formed the 'James Larkin Defence Committee' and planned to get threatened Catholics out of isolated places and into safety. And we took part in marches, went to meetings and watched steadfastly as everything went from bad to worse. But we lived in a triangle that was symbolic in a way – between Coleraine, Portstewart and Portrush, the lines of communication were open and you could live freely, if experimentally, across the divides. Politics grew into Irish culture and back again into literature. We mixed into traditional music and some of the traditional musicians mixed into politics. I started to play in a band called 'Fir Uladh' and we performed at various venues, from anti-internment rallies to folk concerts. It was blissful. And, because I had written some poems, which were published and broadcast, the Irish Dramatic Society asked me for a play. I wrote one – a short incoherent thing, the idea of which I had lifted from Robin Flower's *The Irish Tradition* – and called it *The Skull*. It was duly translated into Irish and, travelling with it, I was proudly introduced once as 'Our Belfast Protestant' to a smiling group of anxious Dublin *gaelgóirs*. We shared a year or two of excitement and confusion, living within that strange triangle.

The people who lived there were mostly hospitable to these students in their midst. Even though our lifestyle was, on the face of it, a challenge to their own, I never heard a bad word said against us, and only once in Coleraine did I hear 'the bigot' come out in a person. He was drunk and on his way home from the bar. The group of us, from all over the North, Scotland and England, and from every 'side', gazed at his ignorance and smiled sagely that his was an ugly old world shuffling off its mortal coil.

The three years did not last long. They were intense though. Everything was – sitting in the campus listening to the news of the Abercorn restaurant bomb blast, watching the slow dismantling of Belfast and the places we used to meet in back home. We threw darts in the university bar, while the literary critic and novelist Walter Allen held court, sipping pink gins and smoking his endless stream of untipped Senior Service cigarettes. Ensconsed in the Anchor Bar, nestling beneath the convent in Portstewart, or in the Harbour Bar in Portrush, poet James Simmons's home from home, there was an air of unreality about the whole time and place.

The people from 'The Triangle', however, lived their lives with a keen knowledge we did not have. They were wise before the event and had an almost stoical single-mindedness about what was happening around them, as if it were a bad season they just had to thole. And us? The lectures went on as usual for those who cared to attend.

I remember in one linguistics class, the distinguished professor, noted for his abstract convoluted manner and celestial gaze, talking us through the derivation of Cornish place-names. Three ex-Oxonians sat midway up the lecture hall rigged-out as 'Red Indians' with war paint and headdress as a bet to show how oblivious the lecturer was of what was going on before him, one of their cats mewling in the aisle.

Such frivolity disappeared with time. The atmosphere became more obsessive, nervous, and shaky. We held together, a generation at sea, but slowly being roped back in by the past. Some returned home to discover that the police had lifted brothers, badly beaten, interned; or a man down the road was murdered, or another Provo bomb had scorched the life out of this street or that, and the inevitable retaliation. Every day was becoming an aftermath of the wreckage from the night before.

The people grew suspicious, distant and hardened. Resentment spiked conversations. Still, we walked the coastline, travelling farther north, west and south, discovering 'Ireland' and, finally, rented a fine house overlooking the Atlantic. My last year was spent there mostly – the white surf from the sea staining the windows, the damp of that big bedroom with its awkward wardrobes and the endless talk tinged by anger, uncertainty and the curse of everything that looked like going wrong.

The previous summer had shown how fragile life actually was. Two of us were going to work June, July and August in the north-east of Scotland, helping to build, of all things, an oilrig. We called down to Coleraine to book our flights and, wandering back to the little station, I could smell something acrid burning. In split seconds, a bomb exploded some way behind us. People came slowly walking towards us, bewildered looks on their faces, calling to other people in doorways and all the while streaming by us. They just kept coming and we called out to stay back, pointing at a solitary car in the road. But they kept coming and we turned into the railway station, stunned a little, disbelieving. In the train, there were just the two of us. You could hear a pin drop. When the second bomb went up, it felt like somebody had shouted out in the eerie silence of the carriage. We gaped at each other as the train pulled out. 'Jesus Christ,' Joe said, 'let's get the fuck out of here.' Within a year, we had all left that part of the country.

Of course, three years does not necessarily tell you much about a place. The triangle within which the university sheltered retains its wonder because of all that happened there. But sifting through those years, I recall a craggy bit of the coast down below High Road when all you could see was the white spume of a turbulent sea and a rake of gulls, thrown up in the wind, screeching to their hearts' content. There was something exhilarating and disquieting about it – the dilapidated hotel with its broken windows and curtains flying out of them; all those tall houses closed in on themselves, as if the people were hiding. Maybe they were. Maybe we all were.

Chalked up on the long and high blackboard was the legend: 'Give us ye John'. It was 1973 in what was called LT3 (or was it 1?) in 'phase one' of the recently, controversially built New University of Ulster. The university was established in 1968 in the unionist stronghold of Coleraine, rather than in the mostly Catholic city of Derry, where Magee College had been part of the Royal University of Ireland (1880–1909) and subsequently had prepared students for degrees from Trinity College Dublin.

A discordant building, it was nonetheless our gathering place with its wide open-plan lounge and 'refectory' where we watched television. Behind it stood the towers and concourse of the arts and science faculties, and beyond them the Bann cut a swathe through farming land, the market town of Coleraine and eventually out into the chill North Sea. A landscape not for the weary or weak-willed; 'bracing' is what it used to be called – brilliant at times and unpredictable, with the Scottish coastline in view on a good day.

The undergraduate students who assembled in that lecture hall were from various arts and parts of Ireland, Scotland and England. A couple of Americans as well. The experiment was straightforward – the last democratic flush of free education that had been extended throughout the fifties and sixties in Britain was now embracing, for various political reasons, the north-eastern tip of Northern Ireland. Build a university there and show that the political union with Britain was still alive, well and thriving. Befitting emblems of adversity. For outside the university all hell was breaking loose on the streets of Northern Ireland. Five years of political failure was turning into five years of bloody, vicious and intimate violence. The headcount was very grim indeed. 1969: 19 deaths; 1970: 29 deaths; 1971: 180 deaths; 1972: 497 deaths; 1973: 263 deaths. Cruel, crude figures never tell the story but spelling them out brings back the sheer horror of it all. A horror that we in our university refused to buckle under; the college life was vibrant, challenging, mind-opening.

It's always unwise to think one can ever speak 'of' or 'for' a generation but certainly the cohort of students who passed through those early years of the new university in the seventies experienced an intensity that is rare. Although, of course, we did not know it then, least of all as we sat there in LT3 waiting for John Montague to arrive and 'give a reading'. We had actually arrived ahead of time and the graffiti writer (mind-blown like the rest of us by *Moby-Dick*, one of the term's key texts) and some other pals sat a few rows back, waiting.

As it was known anecdotally at the time, NUU had turned into a working environment quite unlike (I imagine) what had been planned. The cultural mix of Protestants and Catholics from both sides of the Irish border, Scottish, English, ex-colonial academics, new left, old left, red-brick, Oxbridge, hippy, unhappy, visionaries of a kind, others soon to be disenchanted and yearning for 'the mainland' again. All added to the mix and created an atmosphere that had a truly democratic and liberal energy about it. The college acquiesced as Irish was promoted quite unselfconsciously as a language and culture available to all without political directives; the republican and unionist clubs cut up rough but no one was harmed in the thrust of argument – even at the most turbulent of times, such as Bloody Sunday in January 1972 or after the IRA horror bombings of Bloody Friday in July of the same year. Writers visited the college quite frequently, if unobtrusively: J.G. Farrell, Louis Simpson, Tony Harrison and several Irish poets such as Thomas Kinsella, John Montague and Derek Mahon, who became the first writer in residence at the university. There was a very strong musical tradition being established in the environs of the college, as much as within, fostered by James Simmons, as well as by Liam ÓDochartaigh, through the Irish language groups. The Chieftains played some of their earliest gigs outside the Republic in the college. And here in 1973 we were waiting for John Montague.

Thinking back, it's probably the case that he was promoting the newly published *The Rough Field* (1972), or it could have been *Tides* (1971). If his preface to the collection of his essays, *The Figure in the Cave* (1989) is anything to go by, he probably gave us all a bit of a lashing, one way or another. 'I find the element of self-seeking in the northern [Irish] thing depressingly close to *Ulsterkampf*, when our giant forebears, Yeats and Joyce, have given us the freedom of the world.' While a little earlier in the same piece Montague remarks of Belfast, the city which a sizeable number of his audience that day would unquestionably have called home, that it is 'hard to think of Belfast as a parish, especially since no one has put it on the map. Belfast is of interest as a microcosm of the tensions that rack the end of our century, the wall between the Shankill and Falls a miniature of the Berlin Wall.'

Montague was also none too impressed by the kind of support the North provided for him: 'hard as it may be to understand today [1989], there was no Northern dimension to Irish literature then [the sixties], no question of going to Belfast for someone like myself, when even to get a little *bourse* to finish *The Rough Field* took nearly half a decade.'

Sentiments expressed more than fifteen years after that reading in LT3, but it wouldn't surprise me if Montague did indeed speak his mind that afternoon. Certainly I can remember his first remark, which was an immediate response to the slogan on the blackboard: 'Evangelical', he said, 'is that a biblical request! "Give us ye?"' Which went down very well with the troops in the front row, particularly the Scottish amongst us. The subtexts of that room are impossible to relive now that so much separates us from that time. Maybe we didn't take ourselves too seriously, not really. Anyway, the college bar called by early evening, and that was it.

In the springtime of 1973, the Belfast writer Brendan Hamill introduced me to Padraic Fiacc.

Brendan was, like myself, a student at the fledgling University of Ulster, but he knew just about everyone who was writing in or about the North. Fiacc, he said, was thinking of doing an anthology on the North. I was writing and publishing poems here and there and so, Brendan thought, we should meet.

I hadn't actually met many poets up to that time. In fact, I don't think I *knew* any, so this meeting with Fiacc was important. He lived in the end house in a row of typical suburban houses in Glengormley, on the outskirts of Belfast. His home had been a stopover, at one time or another, for several of Ireland's best-known writers. Fiacc himself had been close to Padraic Colum in New York, where he had grown up in the 1930s and '40s. He was a tangible link between the lost world of the Revival and the disintegrating world of Belfast. Fiacc also knew the work of Joyce (his first book was called *By the Black Stream*, after Joyce's poem 'Tilly'), Beckett, most of the Classics, European writers like Mauriac, Baudelaire, and there was that poem of Derek Mahon's, 'Glengormley' (the suburb where Fiacc lived), dedicated to Fiacc and published in Mahon's first collection, *Night-Crossing* (1968).

After our first meeting, I made a point whenever I was in town of seeing Joe (for he reverted to his real name when the defences went down and he became Joe O'Connor again). We would sit in the living room and talk about 'the situation', i.e. the Troubles, which was turning from bad to the worst it could be; and the domestic chores, which he religiously went through – lighting fires, clearing the garden of leaves, making coffee, spotting the return of birds, putting the 'garbage' out – an obsessed artistic temperament that was struggling with the break-up of his personal and social life.

What was going on in Belfast in 1973/74 makes for grim reading, with nightly assassinations, bombings and this net of fear cast over the city. Every week, one or more would visit Joe; sometimes there would be gatherings. At one of these I met a young lad called Gerry McLoughlin, who wrote under the name of Gerry Locke. He was like the rest of us: a Belfast lad who loved literature but couldn't sort out how it could relate to what was going on around him. When Blackstaff Press published Joe's anthology, *The Wearing of the Black*, I was living in Galway. My girl and I travelled up on 14 December 1974 by train, Galway to Dublin, Dublin to Belfast. The party the next day was the last time we were to see Gerry McLoughlin. He was murdered four months later on 7 April 1975. His murder changed everything and it represented a terrible watershed in all our lives. I turned my back for several years on Belfast and the sickening reality of sectarianism.

One Saturday night in the early autumn of 1974, a squad of Welsh Guards threw a companion and myself against a doorway in the Clonard district of Belfast. This was 'an official army search' and, in assuming the necessary position, the two of us had to part some ways to let the home-dweller through his own door, between our spreadeagled arms. My companion, responding to repeated questions about who we were and what we were up to, blurted out that I did not belong to the area and was, in fact, a Protestant from the other side of town. He thought he was doing the right thing, of course, but the indifferent Welsh Guard perked up and replied, in fierce Cockney: 'A few of your lot copped it tonight, mate. Fancy a trip down the Village?' The Village was at that time a fairly notorious loyalist enclave. He then lifted a paperback copy of Sheridan Le Fanu's *Uncle Silas*, a present I had been given earlier in the day, out of my pocket and, fumbling, dropped it into an oily pool of rainwater. When the officer commanding stepped out of the armoured car, he told us to move on and ordered his men back inside. The book was destroyed so I left it there, swollen with rain water, and walked towards another friend's house some way off, in the lamp-less dark, shadowed by the same soldiers in their Pig. I think that night I decided it was just as well I was moving on to Galway, as it turned out, in a matter of months.

When people talked to me and enquired about what it was like being 'a Northerner', I really hadn't much of a clue. I never really thought of myself as anything other than a Belfast man. Because, even though some of my ancestors came from County Antrim and Fermanagh, and had connections with County Derry, my only real knowledge of the north is Belfast. I went to Sunday school and church, joined the Scouts and lived a fairly typical boy's life growing up in the civil society of north Belfast: playing football, marking every season's changes with a different game, walking the streets, talking and smoking. I had no complaints. The world I knew was the world I took for granted: 'This was the way it was' as Van Morrison says. Our district was predominantly Protestant: we had very good neighbours, some Catholic, some Jewish and other refugees who had married soldiers stationed in Europe during the war. There was a synagogue, grand Church of Ireland and Presbyterian churches, Baptist halls, evangelical Kingdom halls, one Catholic Church, and so on.

The thing that never failed to amaze me, however, about growing up in Belfast was that, once I moved outside it, no one had ever heard of my family. We were, how shall I say, unattached. We did not *belong* anywhere else in Ireland; once out of Belfast, we were effectively in no man's land – whatever about farther afield in London or, histrionically, in Huguenot France. I found this significant because the few writers I started to know something about – Irish writers, I mean – seemed to have connections all over the place. Not only did they know one another, they also seemed to know every town and village throughout the country like the back of their hands. And someone always knew them, too. In contrast we – my family – were, outside the city walls, anonymous. This was not a self-conscious policy, but it was an accepted, almost desired state of affairs. So in my head I compensated: Robert Lowell summered in Donaghadee, portly Wallace Stevens lived up Cave Hill Road, Elizabeth Bishop sat downstairs on the 64 bus, and Constantine Cavafy could be seen, on a very clear day, walking down Duncairn Gardens, minding his own business.

It took the hundred and fifty miles and more between Belfast and Galway to get some balance right; to find a level, and to put things into perspective. This is probably why *The Lundys Letter* and the opening poems in *Sunday School* (1991) are generally set where I grew up in north Belfast. It was not so much the place that mattered as the mood of a particular time there: the mid-1950s and early 1960s. The weight of that world fascinated me – post-war, Protestant – and the dominant view of the Cave Hill, always there, like the past itself, high above us. Whereas the lough lay seductively, promising adventure, and the hills beyond shone with sun and rain. *Sunday School* was, in part, about that world, with its sense of scorn and disapproval; its inwardness and strength; its uncertainty and self-awareness; its survival; its distinctiveness. Bible stories, which had formed a kind of natural moral backdrop to our young lives, surfaced in several of the poems. Life had been 'proverbial'. We were told things through certain parables and I found this kept cropping up in the poems. Some of the poems in *The Lundys Letter* were similarly indebted to teachings from the Old Testament and, naturally, the images, which remained, of church-going and school. But in leaving Belfast, like so many before me and since, I found out what and where it was only after that.

The four lads at the back of the bus were talking. And then the rip of a metal tab as another can of Harp was opened.

> '*The only fuckin' thing is* Pernod *and lime.*'
> '*Na.* Harp *and cider.*'
> '*He's a scar from thar to thar, the size of a fist.*'

My then four-and-a-half-year-old daughter and I looked out the window. This was the last leg of a long, tedious bus journey from Galway to Belfast and the sun had come out splendidly. We were both tired and the conversation behind grated on obsessively. They seemed so enclosed by their own world, violence at every turn of phrase, but when a Christian Endeavour student tried to engage them in talk, one of the lads offered her a swig of lager. She refused and fell silent. I thought she gave up very easily for an evangelist-in-the-making.

Every time I was back home, it felt as if I was inhabiting two worlds, two time-scales, and that they were running parallel to each other. The walk from Glengall Street, now with my daughter and a few bags in hand, and the rush across Great Victoria Street, took me by the site of Sammy Huston's Jazz Club: Frankie Connolly & the Styx, Sam Mahood & the Just Five, The Few, The Interns, The Method, and all those great bands that played there in the sixties and early seventies.

One lunchtime, going down through the cool airy stairway of the Central Library, I recall becoming aware of a certain commotion at the swing doors, which opened out on to Royal Avenue. Making my way through a group gathered outside the library, between two bus stops and the red telephone kiosk, I eventually stood and listened to the clear intonations of a British army officer informing the large crowd on both sides of the street that a bomb had been located in a tailor's shop up the road from us. I knew the building well. It led round to Smithfield Market.

We stood, almost humbly, on our lunch hour, waiting, perhaps silenced, under instruction, irrespective of political leanings, religious inclinations, loyalties or whatever, depersonalised like a group of prisoners until finally the bomb exploded, a mass of shattering glass spilling on the ground, sundered brick sliding across the street to the squeals of women. Hesitantly at first, and then with more fluency, we went our separate ways. But just as the bomb went off, momentarily caught in the shock waves that plumbed the street, I saw a careworn, oldish woman, dressed in the usual sturdy, frayed overcoat and the workaday handbag, suddenly wince as if drowning in the sound of the explosion. Torn by its invisible pressure, she turned in a gasp into an image like that of Munch's *The Scream*. I saw then how oppression works its way right through our very bodies and buries in our souls a physical terror that debilitates and makes acceptable the imposition of any final order. I think I also saw the deadly stasis of history captured in the English officer's poised language, in the blind gesture of violence and the ordinary drama of silently 'getting by' in our citizens' trail of survival.

It's really as if you had the choice of walking on two kinds of stairway – one fast, the other slower. Parallel stairways: this one is the present, the quick lane, of getting around the City Hall to a bus or taxi; the other, slowed to a measured pace, is the past. It's as if, thrown upon an imaginary screen, you can see yourself, going places, doing things, enlarged and selective. Nor is the experience necessarily unpleasant, but rather unsettling; 'a disconnect'. It makes your present actions and thoughts seem transparent, as you look through them to see the past and how much (or how little) has changed. It forces you to focus more often on what is really there, until you get into the way of this double-take.

The taxi-man had a black plastic refuse bag in the back and said he was on his way to the dump when I hailed him. Where to? I told him and off we went, bouncing around, the faces of welcome at the familiar door as the taxi pulled up.

The week went quickly. I gave a few readings in schools; my own school first, at Orangefield, in the staffroom this time, sipping coffee and working out old days and old 'pupils', walking along the same corridors and looking over the playing fields to the Braniel estate. I was still thinking, though, of the silent students I had just left, as they listened to this man talking about their school and the people he knew when he was there, about writing poetry and reading some:

> You staged the ultimate *coup de grâce*
> for the Union's son turned republican.
> I can see you shivering in the cold
> of an East Belfast morning, outside
> school, the bikes upended, the quad
> blown by a dusty wind, and rows of
> windows, some cellophaned, gaze
> back at the encroaching estate.
> ('The Lundys Letter')

Next, over to Rupert Stanley College, sequestered in the East End, with the fabulous crane 'Goliath', like a vast arch of entry into the city. Then Sullivan Upper on the lough side, where an oil tanker edged out on the sea and a plane tipped up into the sky, leaving the coastline in slow motion:

> Deck-chairs gape at the sun
> slinking down behind this part
> of the Irish Sea. Between us
> and the next landfall, trawlers
> criss-cross shipping lanes
> fetching mackerel to Protestant
> villages along the shore.
> ('Resistances')

On the bus back we had just a few on board, returning to Portadown, Armagh, or Monaghan, via a route of small villages all spruced-up and deserted on Sunday. The four young hard chaws weren't to be seen. I sat staring out the window and wondered which stairway they were on and how long they could stick it before they would feel that break in time, fastened for a second, as if the imaginary reel had broken down.

SIX

In 1970 when I was a student at the College of Business Studies in Brunswick Street, Belfast, the college was part of a network of Colleges of Technology and Further Education which acted as a safety net for young and second-chance students to enhance their academic and/or professional qualifications for trade, legal and commercial positions in Belfast's industrial and manufacturing world. It was a world that was by then heading towards decline. The shipbuilding, rope-making, tobacco, linen mills – all of which had prospered during the past hundred years and more and produced substantial wealth for the Northern middle and upper classes – were changing under the tectonic shifts of post-industrialism.

Once one of the very hubs of British imperial capital, Belfast was beginning to experience the first tremors of historical economic movement away from heavy industry and its manufacturing and fabrication bases, but no one was letting on, least of all the provincial government in Northern Ireland, which had other concerns urgently pressing upon its collective mind. By 1970 what would become in effect a thirty-year conflict was barely two years old, as the civil rights movement – initially a middle-class movement of students and professional Catholics with some limited Protestant liberal support – sought to democratise the Northern Irish state, allowing for proper and adequate representation of Catholic and nationalist opinion, decent housing and the stripping away of the worst features of sectarianism, which had blighted life in the North for generations since its foundation in 1922.

That wholly justified and necessary agenda would in a few years turn into a different kind of struggle between various sections of the population and the state – the British state – locked into an appalling spiral of violence and destruction: the Troubles. To the eighteen years I was then, the Troubles was a shadow on the future. I had come from a lower-middle-class family on the upper north side of Belfast's Antrim Road. The district had been home to our family since the turn of the nineteenth century into the twentieth.

My great-grandfather had lived there, married, prospered and brought up with his wife two girls, one of whom, my grandmother, had also settled there, married into a middle-class business family, with some roots in the west of the province, and who had in turn reared a girl (whose son I am) and boy after a period of time living in London and in Canada between the wars. The marriages of both grandmother and mother had not gone well and the two women, separated from the men they had married, established a matriarchy in the house they shared in the same neighbourhood of their own childhoods.

At one time great-grandmother, grandmother, mother and daughter lived briefly in that house, before I was born in 1952. My grandmother died in 1960, the same age as the century. From then on, my mother, sister and I lived in her house until the end of the decade. I had attended the relatively new school on the other side of Belfast – Orangefield, a progressive liberal public school administered by John Malone, a robust Protestant who had taken on the intellectual leadership of a group of like-minded teachers, challenging the somewhat complacent and stodgy educational establishment to adjust to the new times that were breaking ground elsewhere in Britain. Malone's alert intelligence had also issued clear warnings of what *might* happen should the governing elites in Northern Ireland, particularly those involved in the state education of the upcoming generation, not provide sufficient resources, both economically and culturally, to prepare for the fundamental changes taking place in the economic bases of Northern Irish society. Malone's vision was ahead of its time but a generation who attended the heyday of the school benefited greatly from his and his teachers' prescience. Sixty years later the school closed – in 2013 – falling numbers and demographic change the reported causes.

Having sat and failed 'narrowly' as an 11-year-old the qualifying examination to attend the same grammar school as my maternal grandfather, my mother was not quite sure what I should do next. The Belfast of that time could be 'officially' quite an inhospitable place for women who had 'separated' from their husbands; Puritanism and snobbishness mixed with provincial anxiety produced an unpleasant toxin.

Turning to one of her father's relatives for advice, a teacher in another of the city's grammar schools, the name of Orangefield was mentioned as a temporary option. So off I went in the autumn on 1963, catching two buses, one from the north side into the city centre and another from Donegall Square to the east side of the town – Castlereagh and Orangefield in the very industrial heartland of Belfast. It was the best thing that had happened to me, although that first year was difficult, adjusting and feeling the pangs of separation from an all too cosy home life and the primary school, Seaview, which I had attended (and before me, my uncle) just around the corner from where we lived. The plan was simple. I would attend Orangefield for half the year and then, all being equal, and my health held up (asthma a constant bother from early age), I would sit what was then known as 'The Review' and hopefully, all being well, make up the short distance I needed to pass the 'Qually' – the qualification examination. As it turned out, I never bothered sitting the exam. Orangefield proved an ideal ground in every way and I formed lasting friendships there; I discovered literature through the passionate advocacy of teachers such as Dai Francis and Sam McCready, the idealism of civic responsibility and the wider vision from John Malone and those other teachers such as Henry and Moore Sinnerton, and the practice of art from David Craig.

The benefits of such dynamic and gifted teachers also drew in others, in particular practising writers, who addressed classes in Orangefield in the mid-sixties; a bold artistic initiative in a culture that privileged practical work-orientated experience above much, if not quite everything, else.

It was in one of these classes, as we were preparing to sit 'A' (for 'Advanced') level state examinations, that Stewart Parker read Sylvia Plath's poems to the transfixed class. Plath was 'on' the 'A' level course in English literature, included in the set text, the wonderful *Faber Book of Modern Verse* (1965) originally edited by Michael Roberts with a further supplement by the American poet and critic Donald Hall.

Plath was represented by several poems that Parker read and discussed along with other Plath poems which clearly had fired his own imagination, including 'Fever 103°' and 'Daddy'. Nothing seemed quite the same after that. His Belfast accent was faintly inflected with an American tone drawn from his years living in New York where he had taught at Hamilton College and Cornell University in the mid-sixties before returning home in 1969, the year he visited that class in Orangefield in east Belfast – where Parker himself had come from and had his cultural roots, explored in his masterpiece, *Pentecost* (1987). Parker spoke softly but confidently and it probably did not pass us by that he had the look and demeanour of someone who was close in age and manner to his audience. The following year Parker would begin his innovative stint as 'rock' columnist with *The Irish Times* newspaper, producing in 'High Pop' a fabulous record of the musical culture of the time. There was something about the language of Plath's poems which Parker read that afternoon that sounded familiar and strange at the same time – the interrogative, unexpected, staccato syntax; the vulnerability of the solo voice that broaches such trippy heights as 'The beads of hot metal fly, and I, love, I' came close to the music that we all listened to obsessively while chiming also with the anti-rhetoric of the peace movement and CND, 'Greasing the bodies of adulterers / Like Hiroshima ash and eating in. / The sin. The sin.'

Ariel, published in the UK in 1965, was reissued in a paperback edition in 1968 and reprinted again in 1970. I bought that edition in July, clearly transfixed by Stewart Parker's reading and after having completed my English literature examination. Plath became the sound of the time: questioning, self-absorbed, casting her imagined mind in her poems across shifting landscapes of England, New England and the terrible recent history of post-World War II Europe. The English she wrote her poems in – in *Ariel* but also in *The Colossus* (a hardback copy of which I was given by a friend in February 1971) quite simply sounded real, intimate and part of what felt like a cult following.

The English literature examination went well but the other subjects were not up to scratch; however, with a decent clutch of 'O' levels, university beckoned. I took time off, went to London, thought about drama school, an offer of being articled to an in-law's legal firm, returning to Belfast and joining up with my great-grandfather's newspaper, the *Belfast Telegraph*. After the brief London sojourn and hanging out in Belfast, I went back to get the additional grades that would ensure entry into college. So between Parker's reading in 1969, the purchase of *Ariel* the following year and the gift of *The Colossus* soon thereafter, it looks like Plath was on my mind a lot in that final year and a half of the 1960s. Just as things in my own life were about to take a definitive turn, and as the good times were starting to turn not so good in Belfast, I read everything I could of Plath's and about her. Not the sensationalist stuff, but the poetry and the prose and the occasional essay. The year flashed by with romance, dance and nights and weekends spent in the famous Crown Bar, a few steps away from the college's front door.

My mother sold the unwieldy old house in north Belfast and moved to an apartment on the east side. My own connections with the city were loosening as friends from my boyhood were themselves becoming impatient or anxious about their futures and Belfast succumbed more and more to sectarian violence and the social freedom of movement we had known growing up became dangerous.

Some left and moved elsewhere – the gift of *The Colossus* in February 1971 had been a farewell gift. In the May of that year, the brash, intense, somewhat dislocated soul that I was, sat in class with the great historian of Ulster, Jonathan Bardon, as a bomb exploded nearby. It must have been one of the first such bombings which would become a feature of life in the province for the next three decades. Riots had been one thing; shootings, arson attacks, vigilante groups, fights, shouts, sectarian taunting – all that seemed run of the mill. But *bombs* left in public bars, shops and factories were quite another matter. It was obvious, although no one that I knew was actually saying so at the time, that things *were* getting completely out of hand.

The May of that year, as previously mentioned, a friendship blossomed with a girl I had met at a dance. We would attend classical recitals in the Ulster Hall – no Jazz Club this time, my usual haunt – and in that brief time we spent together, barely a summer, she quoted Robert Lowell and from the house she shared with her family in Bangor, produced his books, including a hardback of *Near the Ocean*. I heard more of that contemporary ironic voice which seemed so close to nuances and inflections of what I knew but did not really *hear* in the Belfast out of which I was growing increasingly more impatient to be gone.

I applied for university. To Sussex in England (History of Art), Bangor in Wales (English and Philosophy), and without giving it much thought, Magee College in Derry, a satellite of Trinity College Dublin, which had been in the throes of relocation (controversially) to Coleraine, also in County Derry, near Portrush where I had spent many summers as a boy in the fifties and sixties. The way things were going in Belfast, my unvoiced concern of staying was offset by family worries about my mother, now living alone. Queen's probably made geographical sense. As it turned out, no place was available from the local university since we had not prioritised it as first or even second choice. Bewildered, three of us visited the registrar's rooms and met with a representative who basically left us in no doubt that, in spite of our good grades, nothing could be done. I sat on the low wall outside the university pondering the options before a friend, who had on the instant made up his own mind, pointed the way. The following week we signed on at the University of Ulster.

Along with a host of bright and not-so-bright young things that fate and opportunity and lost opportunity and hope and devilment had brought together in this corner of the last province of the British Empire, the university looked east to the Mull of Kintyre and westwards towards the Irish Republic and the imposing rocky coastlines of Donegal. My first 'real' poem was published that first year. It had been written in Belfast in the apartment to which my mother and sister had moved. Indebted to Sylvia Plath, not just in its original title, 'I'm through', the poem appeared in 'New Irish Writing', edited by the legendary David Marcus and published in Dublin's *The Irish Press*:

It always happens like this
I was told.
First a pain, then a dagger,
And then the room closes in.

I can only see a cross
and a knife—
    a candle,
    a spade.
There are women in bronze,
painted gold, swaying and
    smiling to me.
And men in steel and iron
looking like the moon,
and a priest sitting cross-
    legged like a garden Buddha.
It always happens like this,
in a closed room, like a mouse
skittering about the floor.
It always happens like this,
so I was told.

The poem included in the first pamphlet I published, *Heritages* (1976) and retitled 'It always happens' for my first collection, *Sheltering Places* (1978), was one of several early poems which grappled with the influence of Plath and which, of course, lost out. Plath's sheer unrepeatable energy 'turned my head'. Throughout those early years of trying to write poems that matched or conveyed something of the madness engulfing the places of my upbringing, Plath constantly came to mind as a source of possibility. I was wrong but it was understandable in one so young and imaginatively vulnerable. And in one of those quirks of fate that leave only the faintest of traces behind, in the new university we drove towards that autumn in 1971 one of the lecturers would recount how he had stayed in the same house in which Sylvia Plath had lived her last year.

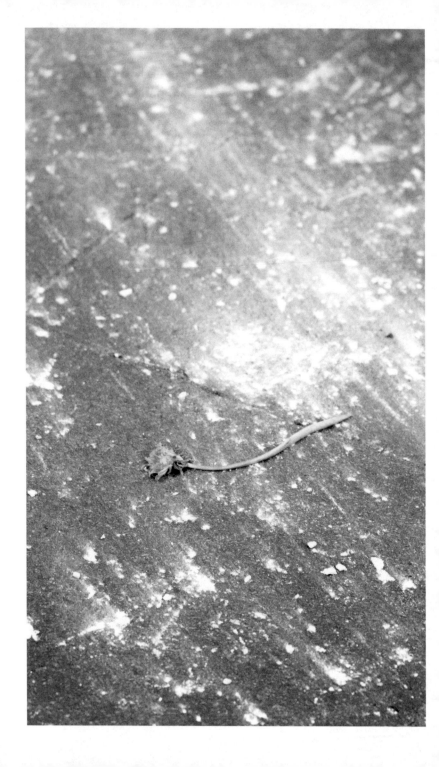

SEVEN

Reading Sylvia Plath took me to Ted Hughes. The significance of his early poetry and his 'presence' in Ireland is often overlooked, particularly on a generation of poets who as very young men and women (in fact, as teenagers) discovered poetry through Ted Hughes. I'm thinking here about how in the early and mid-sixties poetry started to be increasingly seen as a visible form of art practice available on a much wider scale than previously. The reasons for this opening cultural franchise are both large-scale political decisions that were made in the post-World War II United Kingdom.

The democratisation of educational opportunities throughout Britain was hugely influential, alongside the local impact of widely used anthologies in the classroom that stretched beyond national traditions. There was also the engagement of literary critics in broadsheet newspapers, such as Al Alvarez, who promoted poetry at the same time as cultural institutions like the BBC dedicated educational programmes exclusively to poetry. The impact of popular culture included the popularising of 'high' art that saw little distinction between poetry, theatre and cinema, jazz and 'pop' music, as much as there was a new energy leading in the late fifties and early sixties into the rejuvenation of popular arts themselves. Writing such as John Osborne's *Look Back in Anger* (1956), Alan Sillitoe's *The Loneliness of the Long Distance Runner* (1959) and Stan Barstow's *A Kind of Loving* (1960) comes to mind. By this I mean that to a young generation in the mid-sixties, Ted Hughes and others of his generation were seen as realigning the traditional ideas and practice of poetry for those who were only beginning to be drawn to poetry as a form of expression and endeavour outside the classroom as much as within.

In widening the scope and influence of poetry, what it 'did', what it sounded like, the excitement of even making poetry, Ted Hughes introduced new directions while drawing attention to English poets such as Gerard Manley Hopkins and D.H. Lawrence. Hughes introduced city boys to the realities of nature, of the countryside and country life, of the animal world: 'Nature' didn't exist, if you see what I mean. Hughes conveyed to a generation of cool yet avid literature students studying for their 'A' levels, a blast of serious physical encounters that tore into the perceived elusiveness, allusiveness and high drama of what was considered the grand view of 'English' literature. Hughes made us think about creatures and the force of nature not as climate, or cartoon, but as experience. I'm thinking of the tramp and drenched landscapes of 'November' but also the hard-edged pitch of diction that opens a poem such as 'Pibroch':

> The sea cries with its meaningless voice
> Treating alike its dead and its living,

Probably bored with the appearance of
    heaven
After so many millions of nights without
    sleep,
Without purpose, without self-deception.

Stone likewise.

There is a kind of inner ear that young readers bring
to the reading of poetry when first it's new, and the
unimplied terrain of the opening stanza of 'Pibroch'
remains as a tracing of something starkly new and
exhilarating. 'The sea cries' has the sort of rock-lyric
echo most conducive to a fifteen- or sixteen-year-old
starting out to manage different registers and forms of
expression; the local availability of the phrasing, too,
hopped off the page. And later phrasing in the poem,
such as 'probably bored' is one of a number that must
have sounded familiar yet estranged in the existential
pattern of Hughes' poem: 'her mind's gone completely',
'Minute after minute', 'tryout'. We were encouraged
to read these poems aloud in the classroom; preparing
his class for examinations teacher Sam McCready
always stressed the spokenness of poetry, as much as
what a poem could 'mean'. This was the language we
spoke; it was *familiar*.

And here it was, in that school textbook that I have
mentioned several times elsewhere, *The Faber Book
of Modern Verse*. It opened with Gerard Manley
Hopkins, and what a shock that was, and concluded
with three living 'British' poets – Thom Gunn, Ted

Hughes, Geoffrey Hill – and the transformative
Sylvia Plath – only two of her poems, 'Mirror' and
'Death & Co' with the unimaginable lines, 'Bastard
/ Masturbating a glitter, / He wants to be loved'. You
can actually say that in a poem, really?!

There was a definite sense that Hughes, unknown
to us to begin with, other than via his five poems –
'November', 'Thrushes', 'Pike', 'Pibroch' and the
impeccable 'Snowdrop' – was a voice of the present.
The journeys 'into' nature were not some kind of
outward-bound, school-like scouting expedition or
personality-building exercise. These poems were
uncompromising, here and now, reality-checking; piss-
off-you literary-types, the real thing. They made sense,
even though it's quite likely their meaning remained
somewhat unclear, the tone and the voltage of the
language was sufficient. There might have been echoes
too of novels that were being read for the first time,
such as *Great Expectations*, and the opening cemetery
scene of Pip's – or, quite possibly, the cinematic re-run
of David Lean's film on BBC weekend television. As in
'November':

> [...] and I ran, and in the rushing wood
>
> Shuttered by a black oak leaned.
> The keeper's gibbet had owls and hawks
> By the neck, weasels, a gang of cats,
>   crows:
> Some, stiff, weightless, twirled like dry
>   bark bits

In the drilling rain. Some still had their
    shape,
Had their pride with it; hung, chins on
    chests,
Patient to outwait these worst days that
    beat
Their crowns bare and dripped from
    their feet.

In the period that separates Ted Hughes's *The Hawk in the Rain* (1957), the publication of that edition of *The Faber Book of Modern Verse* (1965) and its use as a 'set text' for those thousands and thousands of school students, another anthology needs particular mention, *The New Poetry*, selected and introduced by Al Alvarez. The anthology, published in 1962, was reprinted in 1963, 1964, and in 1966, in a revised edition, included Alvarez's much cited and contested introduction, 'The New Poetry, or Beyond the Gentility Principle'.

Probably best known in power-points by a generalising generation disaffected with the establishment – cultural and political – and seeking out new territory to call its own, when *The New Poetry* reached the Belfast I inhabited, it was hugely encouraging and inspirational. In contrasting Ted Hughes with Philip Larkin, Alvarez probably set the tomcat among the pigeons. But he did capture something of the emotional impatience and critical anxiety of the time, certainly for the young uncertain questionings with which we surrounded ourselves in the Campaign for Nuclear Disarmament, Peace Pledge Union and the Northern Ireland Committee for Peace in Vietnam. Even if, as in my own case, we were picking up the beat a few years later on. In Alvarez's introduction he expounds on the meaning of 'modern English poetry' and provocatively bases an interpretation of Hughes's poem 'A Dream of Horses' on a (dubious) comparison with Philip Larkin's 'At Grass'. But it was the mention of D.H. Lawrence as a poet that was hugely affirming because *Sons and Lovers* was the holy book for the post-industrial late fifties and sixties generation about to break cover. While still inhabiting the working world of manufacturing chimney stacks, factory hooters, and all that went with that culture, the lyricism of the physical world and the electricity of sexual passion which Lawrence renders so movingly hit home, as Larkin would memorably have it, along with The Beatles' first LP.

The New Poetry brought Hughes out of the classroom and into the back bedroom. Along with Thom Gunn, Hughes is given prime billing with eighteen poems included by Alvarez, to, for example, Robert Lowell's six. *The New Poetry* confirmed the opening-up of the 'English' canon to American poetry – as those contemporary American poets included in *The Faber Book of Modern Verse* reappeared – while, curiously, overlooking all Irish poets, not one of whom were selected by Alvarez. The selection from Hughes's first two books in these and other anthologies of the time regularly included 'Wind', 'Hawk Roosting', 'View of a Pig' and the awesome

'Pike'. Although I doubt very much whether I would have been conscious of it at the time, placed side by side the four poems revolutionised how we thought about poetry. But also physically, these poems made one want to write poems, or write different kinds of poems from the juvenile esoteric Yeatsian pastiche I, for one, was reproducing in school science jotters.

Hughes didn't sound so much close to my ear – MacNeice did, and Dylan Thomas, and Sylvia Plath, and even the foreboding Lowell, and then when they really got going, Derek Mahon and Michael Longley. It wasn't a subject-inflected influence at all, though Hughes brought the natural world alive after all those well-intentioned documentaries we sat through in the Audio-Visual Room in school, dealing with the Amazon River or the life cycle of turtles. It was (is) the sheer force of Hughes's English that mattered. I heard it a decade and more after Hughes's critical reputation was well and truly established by the late sixties. But its original impact remains as fresh and as unwavering as when, at the top of a red-brick terrace house in north Belfast, I read 'Pike' and 'Wind', which shook the very foundations of what for me constituted 'poetry'. Later on, one recalls other factors, including the significance of Ted Hughes's contribution to 'Listening and Writing', a series of BBC radio programmes, which turned into the collection *Poetry in the Making* (1967), subtitled, 'a handbook for writing and teaching'. There was the important *Penguin Modern Poets* series which Hughes inspired in many ways, including his fascinating introduction to *Selected Poems of Vasko Popa* (1969), an influence that can be detected in Hughes's *Crow*, published in 1970 and illustrating yet again Hughes's appetite for going beyond the mainstream established English tradition of the time. With the publication two years later in 1972 of *Selected Poems 1957–1967*, Hughes, by now in his early forties, seemed to pass out of view (for me at least) as the Irish and particularly the Northern Irish poets hit their stride and became increasingly more noticed; Geoffrey Summerfield's fascinating anthology, *Worlds: Seven Poets* (1974), with its prose, poetry and photographic narrative cross-weaving through the lives of British and Irish poets, included the rising star Seamus Heaney. Heaney has written eloquently on Hughes's direct influence on his own work and the lasting friendship they shared, as well as identifying quite early on in his lecture, 'Englands of the Mind', Hughes's great energy:

> Hughes's sensibility is pagan in the original sense; he is a haunter of the pagus, a heath-dweller, a heathen; he moves by instinct in the thickets beyond the urbs; he is neither urban nor urbane. His poetry is redolent of the lair as it is of the library.

Somehow this magic-realist force of Hughes's imagination (what he called 'folklore surrealism') that Heaney responded to with such fellow-feeling and which produced *Wodwo* (1967), with its 'sort of half-man, half-animal spirit of the forests', was lost on me. So that Hughes became, at least in my neck of the woods, unfashionable. Until, rereading and rewriting those years as a very young man who had fallen in love with poetry, the thrill and impact of reading Hughes came alive again. I found a copy of the joint *Thom Gunn and Ted Hughes Selected Poems* (1962) and came across his *Selected Poems* (1972) – the edition I had read with such undiminished admiration, bordering really on awe. The memory jolted me when I opened it and discovered on the first page a poem that I tried to impersonate I don't know how many times – 'The Thought-Fox' – and also the stark surprise and absolute wonder of his poem 'Relic', which meant a lot when I moved to Galway and experienced for the first time the stunning seacoasts and amazing countryside nearby. Hughes had metaphorically been there before me:

> I found this jawbone at the sea's edge:
> There, crabs, dogfish, broken by the
>   breakers or tossed
> To flap for half an hour and turn to a
>   crust
> Continue the beginning. The deeps are
>   cold:
> In that darkness camaraderie does not
>   hold:

When I eventually went to college a couple of years after leaving school, I had behind me a lot of reading and a devotee's unwieldy sense of what literature meant. I also had a rather undisciplined idea that writing poetry, and writing about it, was what I wanted to do with my life.

By the time I published my first book of poems, *Sheltering Places*, with The Blackstaff Press in 1978, there was still a kind of naïveté about such things then that has given way to the complete professionalisation and marketing of Irish poetry both at home and abroad. The naïveté extends to the arbitrariness with which I took up teaching. I used to wake up in a cold sweat recalling my first class in 1977 (on Keats's poetry) when I had prepared enough material for a semester instead of just an hour. I remember in the lecture hall, half-filled with uniformed army cadets, nuns and a scattering of male clerics, a Christian Brother, returned from the Missions, sitting at the back of the class smiling indulgently at my crammed and rapid race against the clock and trying to get me to slow down the pace of delivery.

For much of the early eighties I was sleep-walking, living and raising a family, and writing about the west of Ireland; learning about different styles of life and witnessing the saga of the North as it unfolded before a bewildered Republic. That story proved to be emblematic of what would happen elsewhere in Europe by the late eighties and nineties. But the crisis came in 1981 when the birth of our daughter crossed against the anguish and aftermath of the hunger strikes. Where I remembered the common ground of the pre-Troubles era and a determination not to bow to history's grand imperatives, now there was nothing but history, history being re-enacted and debated to what seemed

no particular, defined and achievable political end. I
felt I had to rethink. I began to tap discarded energies
and return to the freer, eclectic roots that I had known
growing up in Belfast and before the dark days had
overtaken the city. I started to explore my own family's
mixed roots, going back generations to European
refugees coming into Ireland, setting up home here
and the significance of that kind of unacknowledged
difference. I was also intrigued by the history of writing
in and about Belfast itself, about Protestantism and its
influence on inherited attitudes to writers; and so on.

The place of literature seemed to be on the leafy
margins of the Belfast I knew growing up. Where we
lived in north Belfast there were, so far as I could tell
when I lived there, no writers: one painter (William
Conor), an elocution teacher (my grandmother) and
piano-instructress (my grandmother), but no writers.
Then, one morning I saw a man in a very dapper trench
coat with a large briefcase standing in the bus queue
and recognised his face from a photograph in the
Belfast Telegraph. My mother confirmed the rumour
that he (Jack Wilson was his name) was a writer – of
novels – and lived in a flat just up from our own house.
He kept to himself and I had heard nothing about him
until I discovered that he had died in 1997 at the age
of sixty. His novels had been very well received when
they were first published in the nineteen sixties. And
as for poetry?

Back in 1967 the head prefect at Orangefield gave
a special class on Seamus Heaney's *Death of a*

Naturalist and we all sat around being very cool when
he quoted:

> Right down the dam gross-bellied frogs
> > were cocked
> On sods; their loose necks pulsed like
> > sails. Some hopped:
> The slap and plop were obscene threats.
> > Some sat
> Poised like mud grenades, their blunt
> > heads farting.

For city boys that was a bit of a culture shock. But
whatever poetry was read during the sixties in the
Belfast I knew, it wasn't Irish. After a brief spell in
London, and on my return to Belfast, a few names
started to circulate: Heaney, Longley and Mahon.
But as to their constituting a group, never mind 'The
Group', it did not penetrate deepest north Belfast.
There may have been some sense that a group of poets
from the North were publishing in London, and could
be seen from time to time around the place; but this
would have been after the event. Not being part of any
literary scene, being turned on by music of the sixties,
obviously meant our minds were elsewhere. Whatever
we read was more likely to come from America and
England than from Ireland and it had to compete with
the weekly order of *New Musical Express* and *Melody
Maker*. For a teenager, living in the middle of a vibrant
sixties' provincial city called Belfast, all this awareness
was for the future.

The poems I wrote back then were about nothing much but a young man's seeking refuge in 'language' only to discover that there is no such place. The poems were written in the attic bedroom of a quiet, tall, terraced house, full of women of various different backgrounds and the voices, of course, always the voices. It was a house on a main road with its back to the Cave Hill, looking out over Brantwood, Grove Park, Seaview, the Shore Road and the Lough – landscapes and interiors, unknown histories in very many ways, that slowly asserted themselves the farther away I went from them.

EIGHT

So the world I knew growing up in the upper north side of Belfast was, as far as a young boy could tell, a stable, work-oriented society. The physical and cultural environment was liberal, non-sectarian and undogmatically 'unionist' (with a very small 'u'); inside the family home, almost exclusively matriarchal, outside overwhelmingly masculine and predicated upon the social and economic priorities of the British provincial class system.

People fitted in to the economic order, having survived the sacrifices of World War II and the austerities of rationing, family disruption (such as evacuation) and other hardships, and looked forward to a better life without the stresses and strains of being part of a society at war. The intensities of the forties had, by the time I was born, turned into the proprieties, as the vernacular of the time had it, of 'making do' and subsequently of 'getting on'.

In April and May 1941 Belfast was blitzed with the loss of 850 people in both German air raids, and large swathes of the city, particularly in the north and east, had been destroyed. Once a key hub in the Allied campaign during the closing stages of the war against Hitler's Germany, Belfast experienced a brief moment of respite in that, ten years later, the processes of regeneration had begun. But, as elsewhere in Britain, the economic engine had not swung fully into action. The early fifties were a difficult time because peace did not bring the expected *immediate* benefits to those who had been at the cutting edge of war – the ordinary people. Emigration – to Canada, Australia, New Zealand and South Africa – in search of employment was common. By the late fifties, however, the opportunities for work and the provision of good affordable housing and education had increased in Northern Ireland. While the management of this upswing was faulted structurally along sectarian lines, in the main the little world of upper north Belfast reflected the changes in fortune as the 'mixed' community lived not so much side by side in demarcated districts, but in random clusters, door by door, as neighbours, cheek by jowl.

Under the surface of this civic society there was a serious and unreconciled divisiveness that spread throughout Northern Irish society – a political and social division which had its own very bloody past and inbred sectarian bitterness. But World War II had temporarily deprived the division of its shocking, defining local significance. By the early sixties there were other overarching possibilities in the air which promised optimism in the future, rather than the fatal lure of a past which had teetered perilously close to engulfing the entire island of Ireland in civil war.

The brief spell of optimism – barely thirty years after the founding of the two states in Ireland and a mere decade or so after the end of World War II – lasted about ten years, from the late 1950s to 1968/69. It was the key formative period in my own upbringing, a generation in which young men and women witnessed the world recovery from global war in local terms. This seemingly stable society cracked open wide in the seventies. In the guise of extremists, bolstered by varying degrees of tacit and/or vocal support, the onslaught of the Troubles lasting almost twenty-five years and claiming the lives of over three thousand people, hundreds upon thousands maimed, both physically and psychically. It left the Northern community stranded and divided in the wake of numerous arduous searches for a return to the social and cultural optimism of the brief period 'before it all happened'.

Two things come to mind as I try to understand this past: to chart the map of my own upbringing pre-Troubles, and to see that life with honesty and (I hope) with poetic value. But also to think about the processes by which we read how 'our' history happens, along with the processes by which it is made, in Joseph Brodsky's term, 'graspable' through the written, the imagined word.

It is a fluke that I grew up *where* I did; *when* is a different story, but in looking over the decades of writing poems and publishing collections of them since the first, *Sheltering Places*, appeared, it is clear to me how a number of these poems 'deal' with the matters I have been describing in this book.

Many more of my poems have completely different concerns and 'deal with' another life entirely in the west of Ireland, where I moved in 1974 and lived for twenty years; living before, through and after the much-vaunted 'Celtic Tiger' in Dublin in the 1990s, to these early years of the twenty-first century. And also responding to utterly unconnected experiences of life elsewhere – in Greece and Italy, in the former 'Eastern' Europe, in America; and writing poems without a local name and often with no habitation whatsoever.

Some poems *are* representative in that they point to a particular time and place and the way that history has made an impact, spotted in the mind's eye, not simply as a remembrance of a time gone by, but as a function of life, with the questioning possibility that certain human values and ways of life are actually inscribed in the very fabric of the everyday. When the everyday changes substantially as a result of violence, so too do those values, which are themselves changed, more than likely for ever; probably gone for good, leaving behind emblems, customs, the look of things, an aura; the realm of memory. I say this without nostalgia but in the clear understanding that certain values may well have been lost; whether they can be replaced, and with what, is another matter. This is the cruelty of time, and the meaning is its cost in human terms.

So the Northern Irish experience can illustrate what happens when the roots of historical conflict, its social and political outcrop, is not resolved in and by democratic government. What the imagination does in part is to try to embody the complexity of what has happened and provide some imaginative form of inclusive redress. But can a common past be achieved or even remembered? The past is not an ethereal thing, it is contained 'in' things and actions. As the German novelist and poet Günther Grass remarked in his memoir *Peeling the Onion*, the memory 'likes to hoard scrap, metal objects promising to stand up to time even in their eroded state'. This is what poetry is – 'scrap metal objects', remnants, relics, vestiges, fragments of memories, in my case drawn from the civic landscape of the Belfast Protestant culture in which I grew up. It was a society ritualised in social customs and domestic life.

Parks and bowling greens, churches and halls, played a highly cohesive and distinctive part in the social fabric of the fifties and sixties, binding together different sections of a community, also marked by characteristically various and independent Protestant faiths, with their own shared social and religious practices of church-going, such as Sunday school, choir practice and the annual recreation of holidays in resorts such as Bangor, Portsewart or Portrush. In idling by any summer's evening, the look and sound of a bowling match conveyed this coherence in an intriguing ballet of formal reserve and response, and simultaneously an intent engagement and competitiveness. The sights and sounds out of which 'Sin' emerges are an image of a time – before the break-up of that society as a result of bitter sectarian conflict – as well as rendering bits of everyday theatre; a game that while played geographically across the city is associated in my mind with one particular park close to where I lived in north Belfast, Alexander Park:

Sin

Whatever was played on the bandstand
we never listened, like my sister's
music box forgotten on the landing
spinning away in its hall of mirrors.

The tennis pavilion, wooden and green,
was for the men – tattooed arms
at the pebbly windows, bye-laws
relating to Parks and Cemeteries.

The tall houses blindly surrounded
the knock of bowls and someone
calling out their instructions
to ladies all dressed in white.

On a bad night the foghorns sounded
like a muffled drum. People kept in.
It'd be a sin to go out on a night like that.
And they watched whatever passes.

Later, when silence fell,
you'd lie there, wide awake,
listening for raised voices
and the passion that cries out of the
    ordinary.

The other side of this composed world was the sense
of mystery that surrounded the faith and religious
practices of 'the other', a respected and detached

acceptance of difference that was a complex of shyness and curiosity which could often turn into varieties of dismissiveness and criticism for what – on the Protestant 'side' – was viewed as an archaic (Catholic) reliance on the undemocratic view of the church on sexual morality and civic rights. Today the situation has been reversed with the modernising of the Irish Republic on most sexual and gender rights, leaving 'official' Northern Ireland isolated and increasingly out of touch and out of date.

When I settled in Galway and had been living there for well over a decade, returning home to Belfast regularly with family and spending holidays in Belfast at home, during summers and at New Year, produced an odd kind of divided self. It was clear that the city I had known had retreated into the dark and inhospitable nightlife of checkpoints, fortified pubs and drinking clubs on the outskirts of town. Fearful of attack and watchful for unwelcome strangers, the social life of the city atrophied. Civilian 'searchers', along with aerial surveillance, streets gated and manned by British army and police, and the endless instructions and security precautions had simply turned what had once been a vibrant and busy city into a ghost town. After a day's work most people hurriedly returned home and shunned the outside world.

I often walked about almost in a trance. Where I had been part, as a boy and young man, of one reality, by the eighties and nineties I now saw another much damaged and torn world. This landscape of streets, houses, shops and pubs of the city I had known without 'knowing' it, was now a haunted and unverifiable place of memories which had become, in themselves, traces of things, echoes; a hinterland of shadows. This transformation from a living past (that is passing away into history) had happened relatively quietly, without anyone actually saying anything about it, marking it down crudely as the 'inevitable' fate of a sectarian and sick society which collapsed under the weight of its own internal contradictions. Which of course did *not* happen.

The confounding situation – so many killed, and yet what was the actual gain fifty years after the first calls for civil rights; was it all worth such prolonged destruction? People will make their own assessments according to their own situation and perceptions of who is at fault, was at fault.

The 'pastness' of the past struck me with even greater force but also the realisation that there still remains a profound and largely unexamined belief that the Northern Protestant community acquiesced in an undemocratic unionism and therefore got what they deserved and so have only themselves to blame. Such a view, which I have encountered in various guises in different parts of the world, is beyond me and beyond the scope of this book. 'The Just' takes us back to where I began, drawn as by a magnet, to the kinds of psychic energy that I hope can renew Belfast and the ordinary life and lives of the city and allow its people to overcome as best they can the seemingly irreconcilable and unsolvable conflicts of the past:

The Just
for John Wilson Foster

So there we were anyway,
in the middle of the night,
driving around looking for this house.
Funny the way you forget the right
    turning.
The last time I'd have been here on foot.
But there it was, the bit of a garden in
    front,
new Venetian blinds, the roof splashed
    with moonlight.

We only stopped for a minute.
Strange how small the windows are
and the fact that somebody's fast asleep
with only a brick between him and next
    door
where somebody else is sleeping, almost
    ear-to-ear!

Do you hear the voices of all those
    houses?
Some are dreaming and others are getting
    by
with difficulty; the doors locked and
    bolted.
Maybe a chesty child is soothed with
    Vicks

or a man and a woman are having the
    time of their life.

Who can tell, coming back and forth
to discuss the place as if it were
    something
different from that face in the unlit hall?
The child will breathe easier and couples
soon sleep the sleep of the Just.

ACKNOWLEDGEMENTS

Looking Through You originated with contributions to the following conferences and publications: 'The Beatles in 12 Movements: A lecture on *Rubber Soul*', part of a series marking the fiftieth anniversary of The Beatles' concert in Dublin, 1963. Trinity Long Room Hub and School of English, Trinity College Dublin, 14 October 2013. 'Robert Lowell and Ireland: A Centenary Symposium: "Waiting for the new life: Reading Robert Lowell in the Seventies in Bangor, County Down"', School of English, Humanities Research Institute, Irish Association of American Studies, the Office of Public Works and Poetry Ireland (4 March 2017) in *The Bangor Book*, edited by Kenneth Irvine (Ards and North Down Borough Council, 2016).

Some sections were broadcast on RTÉ, BBC Northern Ireland, published in *The Irish Times*, *Fortnight Magazine* and in *The Lagan Series*, edited by Patrick Ramsey and Jonathan Dykes (Belfast: Lagan Press, 1991–2015), and 'Laughter and Forgetting: The Afterlife of the Poem', *Memory Ireland: Vol. 3: The Famine and the Troubles*, ed. Oona Frawley. New York: Syracuse University Press, 2014.

To the various commissioning editors and publishers, the author expresses warm thanks and much gratitude for the support going back very many years. The author and publisher Merrion Press would also like to acknowledge in particular Peter Fallon, poet, editor and publisher, for permission to quote from Gerald Dawe's poetry, published by The Gallery Press, including *The Lundys Letter* (1985), *Sunday School* (1991) and *The Morning Train* (1999). To Jonathan Williams, as always, for his care and attention to detail, a very special thank you, and also to Myles McCionnaith and Fiona Dunne sincere appreciation for their work in preparing this book for publication.

SELECT READING

Alexander, C.F., https://hymnary.org/text/each_little_flower_that_ opens

Alvarez, A., *The New Poetry* (Harmondsworth: Penguin Books, 1966).

Bardon, Jonathan, *Belfast: An Illustrated History* (Belfast: The Blackstaff Press, 1982).

Brodsky, Joseph, *Less Than One* (New York: Farrar, Straus & Giroux, 1986).

Brown, Terence, *Ireland: A Social and Cultural History 1922– 2002* (London: Fontana, new edn 2004).

Grass, Günther, *Peeling the Onion* (London: Harvill Secker, 2007).

Harris, John, review of Mark Lewisohn, *The Beatles: All These Years, Vol. 1, The Guardian*, 2 October 2013.

Kennedy, Michael, *Division and Consensus: the politics of cross-border relations in Ireland 1925–1969* (Dublin: Institute of Public Administration, 2000).

Larkin, Philip, *Collected Poems* (London: Faber and Faber, 1988).

Lowell, Robert, *Collected Poems* (New York: Farrar, Straus & Giroux, 2003).

Mahon, Derek, *Night-Crossing* (London: Oxford University Press, 1968).

—, *Antarctica* (Oldcastle, County Meath, The Gallery Press, 1985).

David McKittrick, Seamus Kelters, Brian Feeney and Chris Thorton (eds), *Lost Lives: The stories of the men, women and children who died as a result of the Northern Ireland Troubles* (Edinburgh: Mainstream Publishing, 1999). Revised and updated 2001.

Moore, Brian, *The Emperor of Ice Cream* (London: André Deutsch, 1965).

Norman, Philip, *John Lennon: The Life* (London: HarperCollins, 2008).

Parker, Stewart, *High Pop: The Irish Times Column, 1970–1976* (Belfast: Lagan Press, 2008).

Roberts, Michael, *The Faber Book of Modern Verse*. Third Edition, revised by Donald Hall (London: Faber and Faber, 1965).

Sandbrook, Dominick, *Never Had It So Good: A History of Britain from Suez to The Beatles* (London: Little, Brown, 2005).

Sartre, Jean-Paul, *Nausea* (Harmondsworth: Penguin Books, 1965).

Stewart, A.T.Q., *The Ulster Crisis: Resistance to Home Rule 1912–1914* (London: Faber and Faber, 1969).

Wills, Clair, *That Neutral Island: a cultural history of Ireland during the Second World War* (London: Faber and Faber, 2007).

Bear in Mind These Dead … An Index of Deaths from the Conflict in Ireland 1969–1993. (Belfast: Beyond the Pale Publications, 1994).